What Can You Do with a Major in

PSYCHOLOGY?

Real people.

Real jobs.

Real rewards.

Shelley O'Hara

Jennifer A. Horowitz,
Series Creator

WILEY

Wiley Publishing, Inc.

Published by Wiley Publishing, Inc., Hoboken, New Jersey

For general information on our other products and services or to obtain technical support please con-tact our Customer Care Department within the U.S. at (800) 762-2974, outside the U.S. at (317) 572-3993 or fax (317) 572-4002.

Wiley also publishes its books in a variety of electronic formats. Some content that appears in print may not be available in electronic books. For more information about Wiley products, please visit our web site at www.wiley.com.

ISBN: 0-7645-7609-7

Library of Congress Cataloging-in-Publication data is available from the publisher upon request.

Printed in the United States of America
10 9 8 7 6 5 4 3 2 1

Book design by LeAndra Hosier
Cover design by Sandy St. Jacques
Book production by Wiley Publishing, Inc. Composition Services

WILEY

Table of Contents

Foreword xi
About This Book 1

What Do You Want to Be When You Grow Up? .1
How This Book Helps You Make Smart Decisions 2
Who This Book Can Help 3
A Guide to This Book 4

Chapter 1: Majoring in Psychology 4
Chapter 2: Choosing a College 4
Chapter 3: Making the Most of Your Time at College 4
Chapter 4: Attending Graduate School in Psychology 5
Chapter 5: Breaking into the Psychology Job Market 5
Chapter 6: Career Possibilities for a Psychology Major 5
Chapter 7: Case Studies 5
Resource Appendix 6

1 Majoring in Psychology 7

Choosing a Major 8
The Myths of Choosing a Major 8
How to Decide 10
Resources 11
A Closer Look at a Psychology Major 12
A Quick Survey: Is Psychology Right for You? 13
What Classes Will I Be Taking? 13
A Quick Summary 15
General Skills 15
Challenges 18
The Job Outlook 20

2 Choosing a College 21

Researching Colleges 21
Handling Advice 21
Making Your "Dream" List 22
Reviewing College Brochures and Information 22
What Really Matters 23
Is It the "Right" School for You? 24
Looking into the Psychology Program 25
Applying to College 27

Special College Situations .... .28
    Returning to College .... .28
    Transferring to a New College .... .28

3 Making the Most of Your Time at College .... .29
    Planning Your Classes .... .30
        Double Major? .... .31
        Writing a Senior Thesis .... .31
        Planning Your Resume Now .... .32
    Joining Clubs and Organizations .... .32
    Landing an Internship .... .33
    Doing Volunteer Work and Working .... .35
    Networking While in School .... .36
        Finding People in Your Field .... .36
        Shadowing .... .37
        Scheduling Information Interviews .... .37
        Finding a Mentor .... .38

4 Attending Graduate School in Psychology .... .39
    Planning for a Post-Graduate Degree .... .39
    Selecting a School and Degree Program .... .40
    Getting into Graduate School .... .42
        Preparing for the GRE .... .42
        Getting Letters of Recommendation .... .43
        Paying for Graduate School .... .43
    Returning to School .... .44

5 Breaking into the Psychology Job Market .... .45
    Planning Ahead .... .45
    Preparing Your Resume .... .47
    Finding a Job .... .48
        Published Job Openings .... .48
        Web Sites .... .49
        Networking .... .50
        Career Center, On-Campus Recruiters, and Career Fairs 51
        Find Your Own Job Openings .... .52
    Interviewing for a Job .... .53
        Do Your Research .... .53
        Practice .... .54
        Interview Tips .... .55
        The Interview and Follow Up .... .55

6 Career Possibilities for a Psychology Major **57**

Counselors and Psychologists 58
Counseling Careers 58
Psychologist Careers 61
More Psychology Major Career Possibilities 64
Advertising (Media Buyer) 64
Advertising (Media Planner) 65
Child Welfare Caseworker 65
Employment Counselor (at a College) 65
Hotel Manager 66
Human Resources Specialist 66
Insurance Agent 66
Market Research Analyst 66
Police Officer 67
Psychology Paraprofessional 67
Public Relations Specialist 67
Retail Buyer 68
Retail Store Manager 68
Teacher 68
Still More Career Possibilities 69
Jobs for Psychology Majors 69
Researching Career Particulars 70

7 Case Studies **71**

Beth, Art Therapist 71
What I Do 72
Why I Majored in Psychology 72
How My Psychology Major Prepared Me for My Job 73
How I Got Started in a Career in Art Therapy 74
What Other Education, Training, and Experiences I Pursued 74
What Helped Me Succeed 75
Pitfalls to Avoid 76
What I Love About My Job 76
Things on the Job I Could Do Without 77
My Work Schedule and Lifestyle 77
Statistics About This Job 78
Alex, Sports Psychologist 78
What I Do 79
Why I Majored in Psychology 79
How My Psychology Major Prepared Me for My Job 79

What Other Education, Training, and Experiences I Pursued 80
What Helped Me Succeed 81
Pitfalls to Avoid 81
What I Love About My Job 82
Things on the Job I Could Do Without 82
My Work Schedule and Lifestyle 83
Statistics About This Job 84
Marianne, Forensic Psychologist 84
What I Do 85
Why I Majored in Psychology 85
How My Psychology Major Prepared Me for My Job 85
What Other Education, Training, and Experiences I Pursued 86
What Helped Me Succeed 87
Pitfalls to Avoid 87
What I Love About My Job 88
Things on the Job I Could Do Without 88
My Work Schedule and Lifestyle 89
Statistics About This Job 90
Eric, Corporate Psychologist 90
What I Do 90
Why I Majored in Psychology 90
How My Psychology Major Prepared Me for My Job 91
What Other Education, Training, and Experiences I Pursued 91
What Helped Me Succeed 92
Pitfalls to Avoid 92
What I Love About My Job 93
Things on the Job I Could Do Without 93
My Work Schedule and Lifestyle 94
Statistics About This Job 94
Carlos, Community Psychologist 95
What I Do 95
Why I Majored in Psychology 95
How My Psychology Major Prepared Me for My Job 96
What Other Education, Training, and Experiences I Pursued 96
What Helped Me Succeed 97
Pitfalls to Avoid 98
What I Love About My Job 98
Things on the Job I Could Do Without 98
My Work Schedule and Lifestyle 99
Statistics About This Job 99

Karen, School Psychologist 100
   What I Do 100
   Why I Majored in Psychology 100
   How My Psychology Major Prepared Me for My Job 100
   What Other Education, Training, and Experiences I Pursued 101
   What Helped Me Succeed 102
   Pitfalls to Avoid 102
   What I Love About My Job 103
   Things on the Job I Could Do Without .103
   My Work Schedule and Lifestyle 104
   Statistics About This Job 104

Appendix: Resources **105**
   American Psychological Association 105
   Honor Societies 106
   The American Board of Professional Psychology (Certification) 107
   Other Professional Organizations and Resources 108
      Art Therapy 108
      Sport Psychology 109
      Forensic Psychology 110
      Corporate Psychology 110
      Community Psychology 111
      School Psychology 111
   Other Psychology Associations and Organizations 112
   Journals and Books 114
      Journals 114
      Books for Further Reading 114
   Self-Administered Aptitude Tests 115
      The Princeton Review Career Quiz 116
      John Holland's SDS (Self-Directed Search)—RIASEC 116
      Career Interests Game 117
      Motivational Appraisal of Personal Potential (MAPP) 117
      Myers-Briggs Inventory 117
      Keirsey Character Sorter 118
      Tickle.com 118
   Career Counseling 118

Index **121**

Foreword

What can I do with a major in psychology?

Can you give me a list of jobs I can do if I major in psychology?

Should I major in X and minor in Y or major in Y and minor in X to be sure I'll get a great job?

How often I've heard these questions as a career counselor at a traditional liberal arts college. Concerns about "the major" are consuming to students from their first year through their last. At first it is the anxiety over choosing the "perfect" major; later it is concern that the major chosen may not have been the right decision.

Gone are the days when students felt they could major in anything they chose with no concern about their future careers. Managerial training programs that welcomed bright college graduates regardless of their academic backgrounds are rarely seen, and the world seems to get more and more specialized and require greater and greater focus and preparation from college graduates.

This series of books should ease much of the anxiety around the choice of major through its thoughtful exploration of possible career paths that lead directly from a specific major, or that may at first glance seem completely unrelated. Much can be learned from the personal histories of individuals who majored in particular fields as well as from the rich resources in the Appendix.

Career development is a messy process. It can be seen as a dialogue between the self and the world. It involves interests, skills, values, and dreams. It requires an individual to be able to articulate her or his assets, whether they are transferable skills, abilities honed through jobs and internships, passions fueled by community service—and whatever one has chosen for a solid academic foundation—one's major.

—Jane Celwyn
Director of the Office of Career Development
Barnard College, New York

To Pamela A. Schmutte, my best friend

Acknowledgments

Special thanks to Drew Appleby, Dean of Psychology at IUPUI, for his insightful advice and helpful suggestions. Also, I appreciate the time and input from Christopher Blystone, Assistant Director for Internships and Experiential Education at the Career Center at IUPUI. As always, I'm ever grateful to Greg Tubach for arranging for me to do this project, and finally and most importantly Cindy Kitchel for not only recommending me as the author of this book, but also for her excellent editing and perceptive suggestions.

About This Book

When I was growing up, I had an older relative who seemed to ask me the same questions every time we saw each other:

"Where are you applying to college?"

"What are you going to major in?"

"What job are you going to get with that major?"

These questions always left me worried because I *didn't know* the answers at that point in my life. I started to wonder if I was lagging behind. Should I have already decided on not only where to go to college, but what to study, and then what to do after college graduation? Should I already have staked a claim on my career of choice? I had no idea how to go about making such decisions, and my school hadn't yet provided any guidance. Of course, that was probably because I was still in *elementary school!*

What Do You Want to Be When You Grow Up?

As young kids, we were allowed to experiment—play even—with different career ideas. Did you have a little medical kit when you were a child? Did you build architectural marvels with Legos? Did you style Barbie's hair *and* clothes so that she was ready for the red carpet? Did you use your chalkboard to teach the other neighborhood kids how to spell properly? Did you have fun playing at whatever career was your fancy that day, week, year, hour?

Even then, though, there was probably some pressure. The medical-kit parents were probably secretly thrilled and might have *casually* mentioned to neighbors and family members, "My daughter wants to be a doctor!" While parents might have worried about their safety, they also probably found common kid career choices such as firemen or policemen admirable. They probably liked the idea of little Vincent becoming an astronaut! But what about the child who wanted to drive a dump truck. Or the child who dreamt of being a bartender? Don't parents start to nudge (push even) children toward careers *they* find acceptable?

And the pressure doesn't stop there. The decision of "what are you going to do with life" escalates as you enter your last few years of high school. By the time you're ready to start college, you may be in an out-and-out panic about picking a major. And when you do decide on a major, the advice, judgment, criticism, and suggestions will be even more critical and intense. "You're majoring in philosophy? What kind of job can you get with a degree in philosophy?" Or "A psychology degree? Who hires people with a psychology degree in this day and age?"

As the economy has changed, college tuition and related costs have increased so dramatically that most students depend on varying degrees of student loans and financial aid, in addition to the sacrifices their families may have made to send them to school. These expenses increase the pressure on students to choose a major based on its marketability, not just on their personal areas of interest. Students know that they may be stuck paying back loans for years after graduation, so they feel increasingly obligated to major in something that will lead to a job that can pay the bills. More pressure!

How This Book Helps You Make Smart Decisions

This book starts with this message: Relax! Sure some students know right away what they want to study and what they want to do, but the vast majority admit they don't know—or claim they do but secretly don't. That's okay. You should take your time and really think about what major is best for you, and that's the first main focus of this book.

Second, it's a myth that a major equals a career. Your major prepares you for a career, but not just one career. Your major provides you with lots of varied and different career options. That's the second major purpose of this book: to show you the variety of traditional and nontraditional careers you can pursue in psychology.

Third, the job market has changed and continues to change, and there's no magic major that will assure success. But you can learn how to make the most of your major and how to learn skills that are applicable and transferable to many different fields—making you more marketable. This book also focuses on helping you use your major toward a job that is financially and personally rewarding.

Who This Book Can Help

This book isn't just for students about to enter college (or about to graduate). Many different people can benefit from the information and skills in this book, including:

- ◆ High school students who are starting college and are unsure what they want to study.

- ◆ College freshmen or sophomores who are trying to choose a major.

- ◆ College students who are interested in a psychology major but don't know what career possibilities exist, especially those outside the "typical" line of work associated with psychology.

- ◆ College students who have chosen a major and found it doesn't suit them (personally, academically, or for whatever reason) and are considering switching to a new major.

- ◆ College students who have chosen a major in psychology and are wondering what they might do with this major.

- ◆ College students who are psychology majors but are having doubts and are thinking of making a change.

◆ Returning students who want to explore the possibilities of a psychology major (as a new field of study or as a returning student to psychology).

◆ People in the workplace who are thinking about switching careers and are trying to figure out how their psychology degree can help them in that endeavor.

A Guide to This Book

The following sections describe some of the features you will find in this book. The book starts with a discussion of majors, colleges, additional education, and then careers, but you don't have to read the book from start to finish. Feel free to read the chapters in whatever order will be most helpful to you and your personal situation.

CHAPTER 1: MAJORING IN PSYCHOLOGY

If you have already decided on psychology or are leaning toward this major, read this chapter. You'll learn the basic requirements for this major, the types of courses you can expect to take, as well as general information and advice about this major.

CHAPTER 2: CHOOSING A COLLEGE

If you are already in college, obviously you don't need help picking a college. If you haven't decided on a college, this chapter can help you determine the key factors to consider in general as well as in particular for psychology majors.

CHAPTER 3: MAKING THE MOST OF YOUR TIME AT COLLEGE

This chapter provides advice on how to make the most of your college career (beyond dating and parties!). Instead, you'll find that little things you can do throughout your college years (talking with professors, considering having a mentor, joining clubs) can make a big impact later when you are about to enter "the real world."

CHAPTER 4: ATTENDING GRADUATE SCHOOL IN PSYCHOLOGY

Many majors, psychology in particular, require post-graduate studies. You may consider getting your master's or doctoral degree in psychology. In fact, some careers that might interest you require advanced degrees. The chapter also includes advice for returning students coming back to get advanced degrees several years after receiving their undergraduate degree.

CHAPTER 5: BREAKING INTO THE PSYCHOLOGY JOB MARKET

This chapter contains some basic advice on transitioning from college life to the working world. It includes tips for finding and applying to jobs, beyond the basic "want-ad" approach. You'll learn how to network, use the Internet for job advice and hunting, as well as use career resources through your college (including alumni). The chapter also provides help on preparing for the interview process.

CHAPTER 6: CAREER POSSIBILITIES FOR A PSYCHOLOGY MAJOR

This is a key chapter of this book and describes both the traditional and non-traditional careers you can expect to get with a degree in psychology. The chapter gives a summary of the different types of careers, as well as salary and work environment information. The chapter also describes any required training, government licensing, and other regulatory requirements. Finally, you will also find contact information for organizations that can provide further resources, such as professional and trade associations and licensing agencies.

CHAPTER 7: CASE STUDIES

In this chapter, you read about several people who graduated with a psychology major and who have used it to go into a variety of careers and achieve success. You'll be surprised at some of the jobs these people found as well as how the opportunities presented themselves. In these case studies, the participants describe their jobs and explain what they like and dislike about their work. They will tell you how they got to where they are today and discuss their successes and mistakes so that you can benefit from their experience.

RESOURCE APPENDIX

In the appendix, you will find a wealth of other information related to psychology majors and jobs, including

- ◆ Honor societies, with contact information
- ◆ Web sites that offer relevant information
- ◆ Off-campus career-counseling services
- ◆ Self-administered aptitude tests and where to find them
- ◆ Books for further reading

After reading this book, I hope you find many ways to make a living from a major in psychology—one that engages, challenges, and rewards you personally and financially!

Majoring in Psychology

According to Emeritus Professor Julian Hochberg of Columbia University, psychology is "one of the most popular majors in the country, with good reason." Professor Hochberg points out that psychology is related to many other fields. It is a science, depending on and informing physics, physiology, biochemistry, and so on. It is related to the humanities because it depends on different philosophies, learns from and guides human interaction, and tells us how to deal with one another. It influences many other professions, from standards like ophthalmology and audiology to new fields like virtual reality. It helps decision makers make plans for the military, schools, and hospitals.

As a science, psychology studies the behavior and mental processes of both humans and animals. From these studies, psychologists hope to better understand, predict, and possibly change not only behavior, but also mental processes (for instance, help someone learn to overcome the fear of math tests).

In addition, psychology has many subdivisions and specializations, making it a more complex field than many realize. Areas of specialization include behavioral neuroscience, cognitive, clinical, educational, social, developmental, organizational, psychometrics, and statistics.

This chapter starts by looking at some general things to consider when choosing a major. You want to make sure that psychology, for instance, is a good fit for your skills, abilities, and interests. The chapter then covers what to expect if you do decide on a major in psychology. What courses will you take? What subjects will you study? What options will you have in selecting classes? Finally, the chapter will explore the job outlook for psychology majors.

Choosing a Major

You know what you like, what you are good at, and what interests you. While you may need to do some soul-searching and even seek outside advice, you are in the best position to make the decision of the best major for you. To help you make this decision, consider what issues are important to you, what resources can provide additional information, and what pitfalls to avoid. Let's start by debunking some myths about picking a major.

THE MYTHS OF CHOOSING A MAJOR

Look at the following statements and see how many you agree with:

◆ Everyone but you knows exactly what major—and career—they want.

◆ Your major determines (and limits) your career choices.

◆ You'll just "know" (via a magical sign or omen or dream) what your major should be.

◆ You should consider the advice of everyone when deciding on a major.

◆ You are limited to one major.

All of the preceding statements aren't true. To start, most students don't know what they want to major in; they struggle with this decision as much as you do. Even if they have declared a major, they may be unsure about their choice. Second, your major and your career are not the same thing. Take a look at the list of famous people and what they studied in school (see next page).

As for waiting for the magic sign, it's better to take practical steps (covered next). And while it's okay to solicit the help of others, everyone

Famous People and What They Studied in School

Celebrity	Career	Major
Allen Greenspan	Federal Reserve Board Chairman	Music
Arnold Schwarzenegger	Governor of California and actor	Economics
David Duchovny	Actor	English
Gene Simmons	Singer in band KISS	Education
Hugh Hefner	Founder of *Playboy* magazine	Psychology
Isaiah Thomas	Basketball coach and former player	Criminal Justice
Janet Reno	Former U.S. Attorney General	Chemistry
Jay Leno	Late-night talk show host	Philosophy
Jodie Foster	Actress	English
John Cleese	Comedian and Monty Python founder	Law
Kurt Vonnegut	Author	Anthropology
Lisa Kudrow	Actress	Biology
Michael Jordan	Professional basketball player	Geography
Mick Jagger	Singer in band The Rolling Stones	Economics
Paul Newman	Actor	English
Robin Williams	Actor	Sociology
Steve Martin	Actor and author	Philosophy
Thurgood Marshall	Supreme Court Justice	Dentistry
Tiger Woods	Professional golfer	Economics
Walter Peyton	Professional football player	Special Education

* Sources for this list include www.Indiana.edu, www.Marietta.edu, and Encarta.msn.com.

will have an opinion, but only *you* know what's best for you. Finally, you aren't limited to one area of study. Often students have multiple interests, and colleges offer many ways to incorporate your interests into other fields, the most common being minoring in another subject, choosing to get a double-major, or even adapting your own special "major" (offered by some schools).

Also, if you find yourself in the wrong major, you can switch majors. Keep in mind that the farther along you are in your college coursework and the type of major you switch to will affect how many credits will transfer toward the new major. (For information on switching majors, check with your academic adviser.) You want to make sure that you are switching for a good reason, that you have now selected a major that *is* a good fit for you, and that you understand how switching affects your current coursework and standings.

Now that you know some of the real "truth" about picking a major, let's look at some of the resources you can use to help you decide on your major.

How to Decide

When determining what major you should pursue, consider these guidelines:

1. Look at your interests. What do you like to do? What are your hobbies? How do you like to spend your time? What extracurricular activities did you participate in? What have you enjoyed most? What were your favorite subjects in school? What recurring skills have played a role in your success? When you fantasize about your ideal career, what are you doing?

2. Consider your abilities. Think about your natural talents. What do others say you are good at? Consider how your abilities align with your interests. If you have great talent in an area, but zero interest, choosing a major based on your abilities isn't going to make you happy. Likewise, if you have great interest in a topic, but zero ability, your choice of a major will be limited.

3. Reflect on your values. What do you value? Financial success? Spirituality? Helping others? Saving the environment? If your career and study choices are in conflict with your values, you will have problems. On the other hand, if you choose a major (and then career) that are in alignment with what you value, you will improve your chances of happiness.

4. Think about what it takes to make it in this major and whether you have what it takes. Do you have the skills? Motivation? Ability? Does the major require an advanced degree? Internships? Will you

be able to complete any "extra" requirements? Think not only about the academic challenges, but also about the financial costs and requirements.

5. Look at the career opportunities in this field; this topic is covered in detail in Chapter 6. You might check out the research section of your library for publications, such as the *Occupational Outlook Handbook*. This resource explains the requirements, salaries, and typical tasks of a number of jobs. You can also find links to this resource online at Bureau of Labor Statistics (www.bls.gov).

6. Honestly assess your reasons for picking a major. If you choose a major because it's a good way to meet girls, bad idea. If you choose a major simply because you've heard it's "easy," not a good reason. If you choose a major because you think it has great money potential, wrong answer. If you choose to become an engineering major because your dad was an engineering major, are you choosing based on your preference or your dad's? If you are pressured by your family or peers, you'll end up unhappy. If you just need to pick something, you'll likely make a bad choice. If you choose a major because a job market is currently hot, wrong reason again. What is the right reason(s) then? You should pick your major based on your interests and abilities.

Steven Rothberg, president of Minneapolis-based CollegeRecruiter.com, recommends that students not focus on compensation or employment rate when picking a major. Instead he says, "If they focus on what they're good at, what they like to do, and what's important to them, there's an excellent chance that they will end up in a job upon graduation that will make them happy."

RESOURCES

While you don't want to allow someone else to make your decisions for you, you do have several resources to narrow or confirm your choice. These additional resources include:

◆ Talking to school counselors (both at your high school and at prospective colleges).

◆ Using Internet resources such as interest and personality testing (covered in the appendix).

◆ Checking your potential college for resources. Some colleges provide aptitude testing to help students decide on a major. Indiana University/Purdue University Indianapolis (IUPUI), for instance, publishes a booklet "Step Ahead to Your Future: A guide to choosing majors & careers" (IUPUI, University College Advising Center and Career Center). This step-by-step guide asks students to focus on themselves and indicate areas of interest. From this self-assessment, students determine their interest themes, skill preferences, and personality type. Armed with this information, they can then target specific majors (and careers) that match their assessment. Finally, they are asked to explore and determine a realistic picture of the careers and majors they have targeted of areas of interest.

◆ Taking advantage of the workshops and online information offered by some schools.

◆ Trying the online personality or character testing some schools offer to provide guidance on choosing a major.

◆ Taking advantage of internships or volunteer opportunities in your field.

◆ Talking to people who currently work in your field of interest.

◆ If you are already in college, taking classes in the potential major. While you don't want to spend too many credit hours exploring majors, you can pick a few classes. You can also ask to sit in on classes (rather than formally enroll). As another option, review the syllabus and course materials for a class. Talk to professors who teach a class you might be interested in.

A Closer Look at a Psychology Major

Now that you know generally how to evaluate your choice of a major, let's take a closer look at what you can expect from this major. First, what type person is generally suited for this major? Second, what are the requirements for this major? What courses will you be taking? What skills will you develop? What are the challenges?

A QUICK SURVEY: IS PSYCHOLOGY RIGHT FOR YOU?

IUPUI provides a quick survey of questions to help you determine whether psychology might be a good major for you. The survey asks these questions:

- ◆ Are you social, investigative, or enterprising?

- ◆ Do you enjoy collecting and interpreting scientific data?

- ◆ Do you like learning about human (or animal) behavior?

- ◆ Would you like to interview, test, and/or observe people or animals?

- ◆ Do you like to listen to people?

- ◆ Do you enjoy helping people sort through personal problems?

If you answer yes to most of these questions, your personality is probably suited for a psychology major. If you answered no to most of them, you may want to consider other options or check your motivation for choosing psychology as a major.

WHAT CLASSES WILL I BE TAKING?

In general, as a psychology major, you can expect to take courses in experimental research, personality theory, social psychology, and statistics (for research processing), as well as courses on specific development or psychology issues such as sex, marriage, abnormal psychology, or teenage psychology.

Most undergraduate psychology departments require students to begin with an *introductory course,* designed to provide an overview of psychology's history and development, major theorists and their ideas, and the general methodology used. You'll take a selection of lecture courses (where you listen, read, and learn) and laboratory courses (where you get more hands-on experience).

Lecture courses offer a variety of options, allowing you to sample the breadth and depth of the field. If you already have an area of interest, you may opt for related courses of increasing intensity, such as those connected to child psychology, abnormal behavior, or the learning process. If you haven't chosen a focus area, you can use these courses to explore your options, sticking mostly to basic-level courses in several different subspecialties.

Laboratory courses are also required, giving you some hands-on experience and the opportunity to see for yourself the phenomena you've been hearing about from lecturers and reading about in your textbooks. In the lab, you may conduct experiments with people—including young children—or animals. In the process, you not only learn how your subjects learn or react to stimuli, but you also become familiar with ethical issues (especially concerning experiments with kids), the scientific method, and how to write proper lab reports. To ensure that you get a varied experience, some colleges classify lab courses into different groups, such as perception and cognition courses versus psychobiology and neuroscience courses, or courses involving human subjects versus those using animals, and so forth.

One class you might not think of as related to psychology is statistics. A *statistics* class can help you understand the results of the experiments you conduct and read about. You will learn how to set up statistical models for your research and "crunch the numbers," using one of today's efficient software packages. (Statistics also pops up in other majors such as marketing.)

Some colleges also require psychology majors to take a course in *research methodology.* This course shows you how to structure experiments to get the most reliable and relevant results, as well as how to deal with the ethical concerns mentioned earlier.

Finally, senior and sometimes junior psychology majors take various *seminar, thesis,* and *discussion courses,* which can be very specialized and can give you the chance to discuss your own research, work closely with your professors who are doing ongoing studies, and even get some supervised experience on or off campus. For example, many universities have a clinic—or a cooperative relationship with a nearby institution—and can arrange for psychology students to work part-time with clients or patients. These classes tend to be small, and often meet in a conference room rather than an auditorium, so that everyone present can meet face to face and participate equally.

Colleges may additionally require psychology majors to take related *courses in other academic departments,* allowing you to further explore a specific area of interest. For example:

♦ If you're interested in child psychology, you might take an education course.

♦ If you're interested in business psychology, you might take a business course or an advertising course.

♦ If you're interested in the psychology of women, you might take a women's studies class.

♦ If you're interested in working with a minority population, you might take a history course or a cultural studies course.

♦ If you're interested in treating people with brain injuries or conditions such as Alzheimer's disease, you might opt for classes in biology, chemistry, or pharmacology.

♦ If you're interested in how surroundings affect psychological well being, you might take an environmental course.

♦ If you're interested in alternative treatments used in other cultures, you might take an anthropology or sociology course.

A Quick Summary

The table on the next two pages lists some of the typical requirements for psychology majors. The requirements at your college may vary slightly.

General Skills

In addition to taking classes and learning specifically about psychology, this major also teaches and enhances other life skills. (And it's these same skills that prepare you for a variety of jobs within and outside of the psychology field.) For instance, Grinnell College in its overview of

Typical Requirements for Psychology Majors

Requirement	Purpose of Requirement	When the Requirement Is Fulfilled	Typical Choices
Introductory course	To provide an overview of the field; a prerequisite for all other psychology courses	Usually freshman year	None (although different sections with different instructors and meeting times may be available)
Lecture courses	To gain a broader and more in-depth understanding of various disciplines within psychology	Throughout the college years	Child development, psychology of aging, learning process, human sexuality, abnormal psychology, industrial psychology, school psychology, counseling psychology, and so on
Laboratory courses	To practice experimental research, observe phenomena, and so on	Varies by school	Psychology of learning, cognitive psychology, perception, behavioral neuroscience, personality, social psychology, developmental psychology, and so on
Statistics course	To learn how to measure and interpret experimental results	Varies by school; sophomore year or later, after declaring major	Some schools offer one basic undergraduate course; others offer a choice of courses based on the statistical models used in different types of research

Research methodology course	To learn about the different types of experiments, how to design research for accuracy and reliability, and ethical issues	Varies by school; sophomore year or later, after declaring major	Some schools offer one basic undergraduate course; others offer a choice of courses based on different types of research experiments
Seminar, thesis, and discussion courses	To study a topic intensively, participate in advanced research, receive guidance and support for thesis, and so on	Mostly senior year, with some courses for juniors	Psychology and women, cultural psychology, infant behavior, human neuropsychology, neuropharmacology, animal cognition, motivation, psychology and law, stereotyping and prejudice, game theory, language perception, environmental psychology, supervised fieldwork and individual projects, and so on
Courses in other academic departments	To gain interdisciplinary understanding	Throughout the college years	Anthropology, art, biology, chemistry, dance, education, environmental studies, music, religion, sociology, women's studies, and so on

psychology talks about the school's focus on critical reading, critical thinking, sensible interpretation of data, oral and written presentation, and computer skills (www.web.grinnell.edu). All of these are transferable and valuable skills useful in a variety of fields.

The following abilities and skills are needed to succeed in psychology:

◆ Think critically

◆ Be analytical

◆ Draw from a wide variety of experiences

◆ Have a genuine interest or passion about psychology

George Mason University's psychology department (www.gmu.edu/ departments/psychology) suggests the following two skill sets are required for psychology majors:

◆ Statistical, quantitative, and inferential-thinking skills

◆ Personal growth and knowledge of one's self and others

CHALLENGES

The biggest challenge to psychology students is realizing what psychology is and what it is not. Many psychology majors, for instance, are surprised at the emphasis on math, statistics, research, and other science-based skills. They expect the major to emphasize pop psychology topics such as personality testing.

Another challenge is choosing a direction among the many different paths. Possible areas or paths for a typical job as counselor or psychologist are listed on the next page.

Students who start out in psychology may not understand how difficult it is to become a psychologist or counselor (most require advanced degrees and certification). They are not prepared for the amount of schooling, training, and supervised work involved in becoming a psychologist or counselor.

Also, they may not realize that they are qualified for lots of jobs, within and outside of the area of psychology. The most successful psychology major will look at the opportunities early in his or her academic

Specialty	Description
Clinical	Treats mental and emotional problems
Community	Studies how people function at home, at school, and in the community
Counseling	Helps people cope
Developmental	Studies age-related changes and issues
Educational	Studies how people learn
Environmental	Looks at interaction between people and the physical environment
Experimental	Studies specific behavior problems
Industrial/Organizational	Studies the relationship to work
Neuropsychology/Psychobiology	Studies the nervous system
Psychometrics and Quantitative	Conducts research (college, government agencies, and so on)
Rehabilitation	Studies recovery from trauma (stroke, debilitating accident, and so on)
School	Studies the emotional, intellectual, progress development of students
Social	Studies attitudes and opinions and how they are formed
Family	Studies marital and family issues
Health	Studies smoking, weight gain, stress, and other medical issues
Psychology of Aging	Studies issues relating to aging
Psychology of Law Forensic Psychology	Looks at issues involving law enforcement
Psychology of Gender	Studies gender development as well as issues of abuse

career and then make sure he or she attains the right skills and knowledge to succeed. That's the main purpose of this book: to make you aware of the various things you can do with a degree in psychology and to help you make the most of your academic career to prepare you for graduate school (possibly) or the work world.

The Job Outlook

Of course, students want to know what jobs are and will be available for their major. (That's the topic of this book!) The job possibilities are discussed in more detail in later chapters, but the U.S. Department of Labor Bureau of Labor Statistics (www.bls.gov) lists these significant points:

♦ Many psychologists are self-employed (one out of four, nearly four times the average for other professionals).

♦ Advanced degrees are critical to find work in psychology. Most specialists require a doctoral degree; psychologists in other situations (schools, for instance) require a master's degree.

♦ While you can find a job in psychology with just a bachelor's degree, it may be difficult because many jobs require advanced degrees. Also, the competition for jobs that don't require additional education or certification is intense.

♦ In 2002, psychologists held about 139,000 jobs. Employment opportunities for psychologists are expected to grow "faster than average." This is because these services are more and more in demand in schools, hospitals, social service agencies, mental health centers, and substance abuse treatment clinics.

Despite these statistics, many opportunities are available to you with a psychology major—whether you choose to go on to graduate school or immediately begin looking for a position after completing your four-year degree. This book provides you with information on both of these options. Pursuing a graduate degree is covered in Chapter 4, and career opportunities are discussed in detail in Chapters 5 and 6. After reviewing this information, you should have a good idea of how you might use a psychology degree.

Chapter 2

Choosing a College

In addition to thinking about what you want to study, you also need to think about *where* you will study. What college will you attend? In making this decision, you take into consideration factors related to your personal situation and wants and needs (for instance, scholarship programs, school location, school size, and so on). While you are evaluating the overall school, take a look at their psychology department to ensure that it meets your needs.

This chapter focuses on the general considerations for choosing a college as well as specific information to research when considering the psychology program. Finally this chapter covers some tips on applying to a school.

Researching Colleges

Like selecting a major, you'll most likely get lots of advice and feedback on picking a college. You'll have to be able to weigh the advice you get from others as well as do your own research. You need to think about what college setting would be ideal for you.

HANDLING ADVICE

As mentioned, everyone from your parents to your great-uncle Jimmy will have some opinion about where you should attend school. Perhaps your father wants you to go to his alma mater. Your mother may want you to pick a school close to home; you may want to venture to a place you've never been. In addition to your family, your friends may also have an impact on your decision.

In your senior year of high school (if not before), "where are you going to college?" will be the main topic of conversation among your friends. Your friends are likely to voice their opinion on your choices and may even influence that decision. For instance, you may decide to go to the same school as a friend, a group of friends, or a boyfriend or girlfriend.

If you are an athlete, the athletic programs (and any available scholarship opportunities) may be a consideration in your school choice. You may pick a smaller school because you think you'll have more opportunity to play on a particular athletic team. You may pick a school famous for its athletic program just to be associated with it.

Your high school adviser also may have some suggestions for you, based on your academic performance and interests. He or she may suggest a few good schools to consider.

MAKING YOUR "DREAM" LIST

Coming up with schools you might attend is easy; just ask anyone and you'll get an opinion. While you shouldn't make your decision based on what someone else says, using the advice to come up with your initial list of possible colleges is fine. You want to consider and explore a lot of possibilities before narrowing your choice to one. It's much better to, say, look into a school on your own and decide it's located too far away, costs too much money, or has a reputation for too much partying than to have a parent insist this same point.

So make a list of all the colleges you would consider attending. Then gather information about them to learn more about each college and its programs.

REVIEWING COLLEGE BROCHURES AND INFORMATION

You most likely will start to get letters and brochures from different colleges in your junior year. The mailings will increase as your senior year starts. In addition to those unsolicited college packets, you should write and request information from colleges of interest. Usually you can visit the school's Web site and request a packet of information. You can also find information at the school's Web site; use this information when you want to delve deeper into your information search.

For all the brochures you receive (solicited and unsolicited), take some time to look them over. Doing so gives you a good idea of how a school markets itself. The materials they include help you see what's important to that school. You can get an overall sense of the school and its priorities from its catalog.

Read through the brochure and highlight items of interest. For instance, if you are a cheerleader, is there a cheerleading program? If you plan to participate in a sorority or fraternity, does this school offer them? Look for other facts or figures that stand out to you, such as programs for freshmen, dorm and living accommodations, and so on.

As you review the information, using the Web to find out further information as needed, you may narrow your list to a few schools. If at all possible, you should visit these schools. Reading about a school and seeing a school are completely different experiences. By visiting a campus, you can see the types of students who attend, where they live, what the classrooms are like, and so on.

WHAT REALLY MATTERS

It's good to start with a big picture view of all the colleges and think about ideally where you would like to go. Considering all colleges, even those that turn out to be a terrible fit for you, shows you the range of colleges that are available.

When making a final decision, the following key questions or issues will help determine your choice:

◆ What do your parents think? For most students, parents will be paying for some part of the college tuition, so while you shouldn't feel as if you have to go to the one and only school they select, you should consider their suggestions and reservations about colleges you have picked.

◆ How much does the college cost? When figuring the cost per year, don't forget to include tuition, books, housing, food, and travel to and from home. Out-of-state schools cost more than in-state schools; private schools are usually more expensive than public schools.

◆ What financial opportunities does the school provide? Are you eligible for any scholarships (academic, athletic, alumni, other)? Are you eligible for financial aid? What about student loan programs?

◆ How many students attend the school? In that number, how many live on campus?

◆ How many students graduate? How many go on to graduate school? The numbers not only give you a sense of the size of the school, but also an idea of the success of those students. A good school should be able to tell you what its graduates are currently doing.

◆ How far away from home is the school? You will want to come home; you will at one time or another get "homesick." Depending on your personality, you may be very independent and have no problems going to school across the country. If you are more likely to want to visit home several times a year, take the distance into consideration.

◆ What is the reputation of the school? Is it accredited? You might ask your academic adviser about additional information. Consider also reviewing the college Web site as well as recent articles in the paper about the school. (Use a search tool such as Google to search for stories in the news.) You can also find guides updated each year, such as *Princeton's Guide to Colleges,* that provide an overview of schools. (These guides often include other factors such as whether the school is known as a "party" school.)

◆ Consider talking to current students, recent graduates, and alumni to get their ideas about the school. What did they like? What did they struggle with?

IS IT THE "RIGHT" SCHOOL FOR YOU?

You have a lot of factors to consider, but remember that everyone is different. The school that's best for you isn't necessarily the best school for your best friend. You both are likely seeking a unique experience; therefore, it's up to you to determine what factors are important in your "ideal" school and then see how closely the schools you've identified match.

One key consideration is looking at the quality and opportunities for psychology majors. The college you ultimately choose should have a psychology program that meets all your academic and career goals. The next section explains how to evaluate the psychology program.

Looking into the Psychology Program

Identifying schools you may want to attend and determining the general characteristics are just part of selecting a college. You also need to make sure the school has a quality psychology program. You can use the following suggestions to help evaluate the psych department and its program:

◆ Does the department have a program that matches what you want to do? For instance, if you want to conduct research, does the department have a good research department? If you are not sure what path you want to choose, does the school have a variety of choices? (Some schools, especially smaller schools, may focus on a few narrow or very broad areas of study.) Make sure the psychology department has a program that suits your needs.

◆ Look at the faculty. Do they have terminal degrees (that is, did they finish their doctorate or master's degree)? Is the faculty still active in publishing and research? Will you have the opportunity to do research with faculty members? If the department lacks research or publishing activity, it may not be as cutting-edge or current as you need.

◆ Who teaches the classes? If the faculty is busy with research and publishing, you may have adjunct faculty doing the bulk of teaching. This isn't necessarily a bad thing; often the adjunct faculty is very good and has real-world experience. If you select a college because you want to study with a particular professor, however, make sure that professor personally teaches the classes.

◆ What is the student-to-faculty ratio? Will you be able to get individual attention and advice? This consideration is especially important when you need help landing an internship or shadowing a professional in the field, or if you are seeking a mentor (all topics covered in the next chapter). Can you make contact with someone in the psychology department (versus just admission) when you are applying to or evaluating the school?

◆ What activities, organizations, and clubs does the psychology department or school support? At the school's Web site, check out the page for the department and get a sense of the opportunities available.

◆ What type of career advising is available and who does the advising? Professors in the psychology department? Faculty advisers? Does the school hire professional advisers? Use peer advisers? A combination? What background do these counselors have? For the best advice, you may consult with several or all of these types of advisers. You want someone who has experience working in that field. That might be the faculty, outside consultants, or even professional advisers. Other types of counselors can still provide helpful information. Students or peer advisers may provide a student perspective of the major, which is worthwhile when thinking about your major or dealing with problems that occur with your major.

◆ Psychology covers a vast range of studies, and some schools adhere to a certain field or aspect of psychology. Is the program centered on behaviorists? Psychodynamic, for instance?

◆ Visit some psychology classes, if possible. How active are the students? How effective is the professor? Would you be challenged by this class?

◆ Find out if the psychology department has a course that will help you determine what you can do with a degree in psychology. This type of course is becoming more popular because it not only shows students what is possible with a degree in psychology, but also lets them know what skills and experiences they need to get during college in order to get that job after graduation.

◆ See if the department keeps track of where their alumni are employed or where they have gone to graduate school. A department that is committed to the success of its students often follows up to see how well they are doing in the real world—versus patting them on the back and letting them go after graduation.

Where can you find this information? By reading through department publications.

You can also find information on the college Web site, from talking with those in the psychology department, from talking to other students, and from talking to faculty. You may also consider talking with some alumni from the school.

Applying to College

After you have decided on a college, you assemble your application. Schools vary, but most require scores from a college entrance exam (either the SAT or the ACT, depending on the school), a college application, and your transcripts from high school. On the application, you'll most likely be asked to list your high school activities. Think hard about your involvement in school, athletics, work, and hobbies. Just because you were not class president does not mean you don't have applicable skills and experiences that you can use to illustrate your better qualities. Perhaps you worked part-time throughout high school. If so, what were your responsibilities? Look for the transferable skills (rather than the task). Stress that you were responsible for balancing the sales income and transactions, for example, rather than writing that you "cleared the registers." Include any volunteer work or service hours you completed (high schools are starting to require this type of community involvement).

You'll also have to write a letter or essay, perhaps answering a specific question. (Again the actual application will vary depending on the college.) Spend some time on this element. Organize your thoughts. Make clear points. Edit and proofread for mistakes. Think of this as one of your most important graded writing assignments!

You may also attend an admittance interview or have to meet other requirements to apply. Some schools also enable you to apply online (and to track your application online). Check with your high school guidance counselor for help with application questions. If your counselor can't help, check the college's Web site, which may include a list of frequently asked questions about applications. And if you are still stumped, call the admissions office directly. You want to make sure your application isn't overlooked or dismissed because you forgot or incorrectly filled out a required element.

Special College Situations

If you are returning to college or transferring from another college, review the advice in this section to help with your particular situation.

RETURNING TO COLLEGE

If you are returning to college from work or from raising a family, you'll need to go through the same process of deciding what criteria define an ideal college for you, researching colleges, looking into the psychology department, and applying for college. You may be more limited because of family, work, location, or financial concerns.

Depending on your situation, you may have different needs or stress different aspects of the college environment. For instance, if you have young children, you may want to see whether the school offers daycare facilities. If you are working and going to school, look for a school that has flexible class scheduling, such as night courses. Some schools offer these classes off-campus at convenient sites such as high schools or shopping malls. You may also look into online schools, but be sure they are accredited. You may want a school with a diverse student body (perhaps with older or returning students rather than just the typical students aged 18 to 22+ years).

Check with admissions to see whether past college credits can still be applied toward your degree.

TRANSFERRING TO A NEW COLLEGE

If you are transferring, you'll go through the same process of identifying and selecting a new college. Because you've already been to college, articulate what worked and what didn't work about your last college experience. Why are you transferring? What are you seeking in your new school?

As for the classes you have already taken, check with admissions to see whether the credits will transfer. This may take some haggling. For instance, you may have to show how two classes are essentially the same although they have different names. Try to find an ally on your new campus who can help steer you through the transfer process. That person might be from the admissions office or from the psychology department. You may also seek help from the academic and career counseling center.

Making the Most of
Your Time at College

Your time at college will go by quickly, and if you think only studying the material and making decent grades will help you succeed, you are wrong. Employers don't really care if you can recite a timeline of Freud's publishing (unless you are going to be hired as a Freud historian); they care what you have experienced, perhaps writing a senior thesis showing your effective writing style, perhaps doing research, perhaps being a mentor to incoming students. What you get involved in and what you do with your time are just as—if not more—important than the content you learn in the classes you take.

That's not to say that you shouldn't study or learn the material in your classes; what it does say is that if you want to graduate and get a job or go on to graduate school, you have to start making plans during your entire college career, not just that last year or semester. This chapter focuses on the many ways that as a psychology major you can maximize your college experience so that you can find success when you finish your degree. (Chapters 4 and 6 cover where to find and continue that success, whether in graduate school or the working world.)

This chapter focuses on getting the most from your classes, exploring career possibilities early in your college experience, and taking advantage of real-world opportunities such as internships and job shadowing. Networking while in college is also covered. Networking after school is critical to finding a job, but you should start learning and using this skill while you are in college.

Planning Your Classes

Most employers and graduate programs aren't interested in the content you know. They want to know what skills you have acquired, in particular what social skills. Can you work with a team? Get along with a diverse group of people? Take the initiative? Be persistent? (This follows the same list of characteristics that most employers seek; this list is covered in Chapter 5.)

The most important goal is to have some understanding of what you want to do. If you want to be a counselor, you should look at what Dean Appleby of IUPUI calls the "KSCs" or the knowledge, skills, and characteristics required for that field. Your major course work will be determined by the path you select, but you can then add to this knowledge by a careful choice of a minor and electives. For instance, if you want to use your psychology degree to get a job in advertising (that's a common path), you might get a minor in advertising or take courses in marketing research and analysis. If you want to use your psychology degree to work as a school counselor, you may want to take education classes.

If you aren't sure what skills a particular path requires, look into it in more depth. (Chapters 6 and 7, for instance, introduce some common and not-so common paths pursued by psychology majors.) You can also ask your college career department for advice. If they know what you are interested in, they can guide you toward classes that fit that interest and build particular skills. Faculty members are another great resource for making recommendations on minors or other electives to take as part of your complete degree.

One thing to keep in mind: If you hate a particular class, consider viewing that dislike in a different light. For instance, if you hate math and put it off until the very end, are you going to be very competitive compared to students who are more well rounded (and didn't avoid math as much as possible)? If you have a weakness, it might be a better idea to try to build up that area rather than ignore it. You don't have to strive to be a star, but at least think about taking another class in that subject so that you are comfortable and more confident.

DOUBLE MAJOR?

Should you get a double major? Only if you think it's critical to succeed in the particular field you are interested in. For instance, if you are keen on counseling immigrants new to America, you might pursue an additional major in a language (Spanish, for instance). You may decide to minor in English as a Second Language as another option.

The bottom line is that there's not some magical combination of classes/majors/minors for psychology majors. There's just the combination that's right for you and what you want to pursue.

WRITING A SENIOR THESIS

Your program may require you to write a senior thesis. This requirement will vary from program to program and from school to school. You should know the exact requirements of your major from the very beginning so something big—like a senior thesis—doesn't sneak up and take you by surprise!

Some ways to use your senior thesis to help prepare for your future in psychology include writing your paper on your career field or writing a paper that involves research or synthesis on a key issue related to your career of interest.

For instance, you can ask to write your paper on a career interest. Suppose that you are interested in the field of experimental psychology. What does it involve? Where are the challenges in this field right now? What are the job opportunities? What is the outlook? How is this field changing the way we live? Answering these questions not only creates an interesting paper, but also lets you focus your school work on a useful topic—learning more about one of your possible career interests.

As another idea, think about how potential employers might view your topic. For instance, if you are interested in counseling the elderly, focus your thesis on the demographic rise of the elderly and the social service and government programs that this population will need. This research and the resulting paper will provide you with information as well as experience (you'll most likely talk to that age group) in dealing with the elderly. If you then use your psychology degree to apply as a retirement activity coordinator (or some other job within this area), your employer is likely to look favorably on not just the paper, but the initiative to explore this topic as well as the knowledge and experience gained.

In addition to your academic studies, look at the other opportunities to gain experience (and have fun and meet people) at your school.

PLANNING YOUR RESUME NOW

It may seem a little premature, but you might consider starting your resume your freshman year. One dean of psychology suggests including the likely headings you'll need for a solid resume. This dynamic tool lets you know what's necessary and what you need to do over the next few years. You have a plan so that you can fill in the requirements as you go. If you know you want to do social work and that work requires experience with a marginalized population, for instance, then look for some way to volunteer or otherwise work with this type of person. Your experience then reflects the requirements of your career or field of interest. Also consider planning your classes for all four years of college, and using the resume and the class plan as dynamic tools to chart your progress and make changes as needed. (You might, for example, decide after doing social work that you don't have the patience for it, so you change to a different area of psychology.)

Joining Clubs and Organizations

Take advantage of campus activities and organizations. Participating in activities and joining organizations helps you meet others in the field— also called *networking*. You can also use this as a chance to expand your experience, perhaps by participating in a club. These experiences also help you build skills useful for the job market. Even if they aren't related to psychology, these activities can be a bonus. If you are the events planner for your sorority and you want to work in a non-profit organization, for example, you could show how your event-planning skills are a perfect match for some requirements of that field.

Also, get involved in the psychology department's activities; these may include signing guest speakers, planning receptions and seminars, and working on committees. You may want to attend an academic conference that is held at your school or nearby.

Look into the psychology clubs or organizations on your campus and get involved. You may join the National Honor Society in Psychology (Psi Chi), which has activities to help students network with professors and professionals in the field. From these relationships, you may become involved in writing research projects, completing an internship, shadowing a job, and more. These connections then become a good source of letters of recommendation (for applying to graduate school or for applying to get a job). Psi Chi also offers other benefits including a quarterly newsletter and participation in regional and national psychological association meetings. (See the appendix for more about this organization.) Check to see whether your campus has a chapter of Psi Chi—or any other psychology clubs.

As another possibility for gaining experience, you may volunteer to help with department activities. Or your psychology department may have part-time employment opportunities. Another idea is to check with the career center for job or volunteer opportunities; you may want to be a mentor to new students, for instance. Or you may apply for a position living in a dorm as the housing coordinator or resource.

Clubs and campus activities offer some great ways to get involved. When you apply to graduate school or for a job, you can use these experiences to show the skills, characteristics, or knowledge you gained. In addition, look at more formal opportunities to explore different careers and gain experience. These include internships and volunteer work, covered next.

Landing an Internship

Internships are a key way to gain experience and information. Participating in an internship provides you with real-world experience, making you more attractive to graduate schools or employers. If you participate in an internship, you gain many benefits. First, the experience can help you fine-tune your career path. After participating in an internship, you may end up saying, "Yes, this is something I want to do!" On the other hand, the experience may end with you deciding, "I thought I wanted to be a counselor, but I have no patience. This is *not* the career for me." It's much better to find out this information now rather than *after* you graduate and pursue all the accreditation, advanced schooling, or job searching necessary to get you into a specific career, only to find you're not suited for it.

In addition to enabling you to "test drive" a career, an internship gives you relevant job experience to include on your resume. You not only learn more about that particular field, but you also gain a job reference. This leads to more benefits when you are seeking a job. If you participate in an internship, studies have shown you are more likely to find a job in that particular area, you're likely to receive more job offers after graduation, and you may receive a higher starting salary when you do find a job.

You should participate in at least one internship during your undergraduate psychology studies. You'll find ample opportunities, as described in the next section.

Sources for finding internships in general and specifically in psychology include the following:

◆ Become a teaching assistant or take some role in a mentoring capacity for other students. You can find these opportunities as both an undergraduate and graduate student.

◆ Check out non-profit organizations. These organizations often use interns as temporary staffing. To find non-profits, check out online resources, look in the phone book, and check with the chamber of commerce. See whether they have any internship or volunteer opportunities.

◆ Look up the social services organizations in your area and ask if they have any available internships or volunteer positions. Because these organizations often have very small budgets, they often offer internships and volunteer opportunities. Some example organizations include Domestic Violence Alternatives and Young Women's Resource Center.

◆ Check with your career center, which will usually have information about internships available. Some psychology departments require internships (practicum) and set them up for the students. In addition to the department, look at the school level. For instance, you may check into the school of science (if psychology is housed within the school of science) for internship opportunities.

◆ Use your library and find one of the many guides to internships, including *The Internship Bible*, *Best 110 Internships*, and *Peterson's Internship Guide*. *Peterson's Internship Guide* lists internships by field and includes general information, benefits, and contact information. Unfortunately, the guide does not include a topic called "Psychology"; for relevant internships try starting with the General category under Professional, Scientific, and Technical Services.

◆ Visit Web sites to check for internships. You may look by area, organization, or career. If you are interested in using your psychology degree in connection with politics (as a lobbyist, for instance), you may want to find an internship in Washington, D.C. Try these sites: www.dcinternship.org, www.twc.org, and www.washington internship.com. If you want to use your psychology major to work with youth development agencies, visit the National Assembly, which provides a directory of internships in these agencies (www. nassambly.org).

◆ If you are interested in working for a particular company, check with that company. Many company Web sites list internships. You can also call the human resources department to ask about opportunities.

◆ Check with the career center or alumni association at your college. Many alumni have volunteered to be mentors, to provide shadowing opportunities, or to schedule information interviews about their career. Alumni are an underused resource. In addition to mentoring and information, they may also be able to help you find an internship.

Doing Volunteer Work and Working

You may also consider doing volunteer work; psychology especially offers many opportunities for volunteering. For instance, you may volunteer with a suicide prevention, teenage runaway, or AIDS counseling hotline. You may serve as a research assistant for a graduate student seeking a Ph.D. or other degree. You may volunteer as a camp counselor or for programs that work with emotionally disturbed or developmentally delayed kids.

Like an internship, volunteer work gives you the chance to actually work in the field; this can help you determine if it's a field you want to pursue. Second, you gain valuable experience. Third, you also meet people who can add to your network.

You may also look for a part-time job that includes relevant skills. For instance, look for a job with the admissions office. The office usually uses students to give tours to visiting students and parents. Look for part-time work positions within the psychology department.

Networking While in School

When you are in college, begin to explore the different career paths of interest. You can learn more about a career by getting information from your career center, but often the best place for information is from people who actually perform the job. You can take advantage of resources at the career center and your school to start networking while still in school. Doing so provides you with the opportunity to learn more about different careers as well as to make important connections.

FINDING PEOPLE IN YOUR FIELD

You have several sources available for finding people who work in your field of interest or who can help you learn more about finding a career with a psychology degree. First, start at the career center. They should have access to employers and alumni, as well as to students who have recently participated in an internship or recently found work. You can identify jobs of interest (if you already have some idea of the career you want to pursue) and see if the career center can find a match. Or you can ask the career center to put you in touch with people who graduated with a psychology degree and are now working.

Alumni are a great source for information. You share a connection with these people: your school! They are likely to want to help you. You can ask them for information about careers of interest. Or you might ask your school for a list of alumni with psychology degrees and see what jobs they currently hold. Rutgers, for instance, lists recent graduates in psychology as well as their job titles on their Web site (www. rutgers.com).

Other sources include faculty, parents, friends of parents, and parents of friends. All of these people are sources of networking connections. From these sources, you might seek to shadow a job, set up an information interview, or even find a mentor.

SHADOWING

One way to investigate a career to see if you like it and to make valuable connections is to shadow. Your school may have some organized shadowing programs. For instance, shadowing is common in medical and dental school. Check with your career center to see if they have a list of practicing professionals who are available for shadowing. If your career center doesn't have a shadowing program or list, you may need to make the connections yourself. In this case, if you meet someone who has a career you think you might like to pursue, ask if you can shadow him or her for a day (or morning or afternoon). Most people are honored to help, and if they say no, you can try someone else.

When shadowing, don't interfere with the person's workday and schedule. Remain in the background, as an observer. You should, though, at some time get a chance to talk to that person about that career. If so, ask the person about the job. (See the list of questions for an information interview below for more ideas about questions to ask.)

SCHEDULING INFORMATION INTERVIEWS

When you do make a connection with someone with a job of interest or who has put his or her psychology degree to good use, be prepared to ask that person questions to help you on your career path. You can also set up these information interviews as a way to gather information (and make contacts) with those in the field.

Make sure when you are talking about careers that you are not asking the person for a job. You are just asking questions *about* the job. Find out how people in that particular field typically get their start and what path their career follows from there. For instance, what's the typical starting job title? What are the promotions or paths from that field? Ask, "How did you get your start? What did you do next? What went well in your career so far? What would you do differently if you could do it over?" Most people are happy to share their story.

In addition to finding out specific ways to gain entry into a career, ask questions to find out more about the career itself. Ask questions such as, "What do you like best about your job? What do you dislike? What are your daily duties? Work hours? What are people in this field like? What skills do you need to succeed in this career?"

Finally, ask them for other resources and information you may not have thought of. Ask, "What other advice do you have for me to get started? What haven't I asked that I should have?" And finally, be sure to ask for other networking leads. Ask, "Can you tell me someone else I might talk to?"

After the interview, be sure to send a thank-you note, handwritten or typed (not email). Little courtesies like this go a long way in establishing a relationship with those people you meet in your career exploration.

FINDING A MENTOR

Through information interviews, internships, and participating in activities, you may be lucky enough to hook up with a mentor. A mentor is someone, usually a professional already established in a psychology field, who takes a special interest in you and helps you make connections, writes letters of recommendations, arranges interviews and internships, and gives you advice on what classes to take or where to go to graduate school.

Having a mentor can be like having a fairy godmother, so it's worth your effort to seek a willing professional to help you. You can find a mentor by talking to faculty, perhaps through an internship, or through the alumni office. Keep in mind that many alumni have signed up to be mentors but are never called; this is an underused resource for finding a mentor. Finally, you may simply identify someone whom you want to model your career on and just ask that person to be your mentor.

Chapter 4

Attending Graduate School in Psychology

According to the 1999 version of *The College Majors Handbook,* nearly 40% or more psychology majors earn post-graduate degrees. This number varies depending on the school.

The decision to attend graduate school, for the most part, depends on your aspirations. If you want to be a counselor, for instance, you must attend graduate school because a post-graduate degree is required. On the other hand, if you want to work in advertising, you don't need an advanced degree.

This chapter looks at the opportunities graduate school offers as well as explains how to select a graduate school and program and how to apply for graduate school. Finally, this chapter discusses some specific resources you can use to find additional information about these topics.

Planning for a Post-Graduate Degree

The following careers require a graduate degree and usually some sort of certification (this varies from state to state): school or educational psychologist, clinical or counseling psychologist, researcher, professor, social worker, social psychologist, and social services director. Also, some students get a psychology major and then go on to law, medical, or veterinarian school; all of these careers require advanced degrees and training.

If you plan to pursue graduate school, you need to complete the following:

♦ During your junior year, start researching graduate schools of interest.

♦ Plan to take the GRE (Graduate Entrance Exam). It's best to take this test in your junior year, but you can also take it during your senior year.

♦ Submit your application for graduate school.

You'll find more detailed information about each of these steps in this chapter.

Selecting a School and Degree Program

If you are in college, you likely are already familiar with the steps on how to research a school. You follow the same basic procedure when looking into a graduate program that you followed when looking into your undergraduate school. Consider these strategies for finding out information about the many available programs:

♦ Check out the school's Web site to see what their graduate program offers. Does it meet your needs? Does it have enough diversity or options? What if you change your focus? Is the program flexible?

♦ Look into the faculty at the college. Does the school include any key faculty? For instance, if you are interested in a particular research topic within psychology, does the school have the leading expert in that field? If so, this will likely affect your decision.

♦ Look at the activities of the faculty. What percentage of faculty is doing research? What faculty members are publishing? Are the programs you are interested in actively pursuing new information? You obviously don't want to choose a program that is stagnant within the department. If the program you're interested in isn't actively researching and publishing, but other programs are, you might want to rethink the school.

◆ Ask your department head, faculty you admire at your existing college, alumni, and other networking connections for recommendations. For instance, where did your favorite professor pursue his graduate degree(s)?

◆ If possible, visit the graduate schools that interest you. Also, talk to students in each school's graduate program. See if you can get a sense of the "climate" of each school—what fields of psychology are stressed?

◆ Look into mentoring and career advising resources. Will you be able to find a mentor? Internship? Career advice? See what resources both the career center and the psychology department offer.

◆ Determine what activities and opportunities are available for graduate students. Does the campus have an active branch of the Psychology Honor Society (Psi Chi)? What other graduate psychology activities are available?

◆ Check out what campus positions are available to provide you with real-world experience. For instance, does the school have a mentoring program where you can mentor incoming students?

◆ Visit sites dedicated to reviewing or discussing graduate schools. Some sites include www.gradschool.com or graduateguide.com. www.gradschool.com includes links to graduate schools (mostly those with online graduate programs). The GRE page contains links for test preparation sites (that charge fees). graduateguide.com enables you to search for a school by keyword, major, or state. You can then review the list of schools and get information about each of the schools and their psychology graduate programs.

◆ Make sure your graduate program and school are accredited. (graduateguide.com includes an article on the importance of accreditation as well as resources to find out if your school is accredited.)

◆ The APA publishes a magazine, *gradPSYCH,* for graduate students. You can get an idea of the contents as well as subscription information at gradpscyh.apags.org.

Getting into Graduate School

Applying for graduate school is similar to applying for college, only the graduate school admittance committee is looking for a more experienced, learned student. The stakes are higher, but the requirements are very similar.

In particular, the gradate school will most likely review the following:

◆ Your undergraduate grade point average (GPA) and your transcript. The committee will look at what courses you took, whether you showed improvement over your school career, whether your course work has any gaps or holes, and whether your course work shows planning for your specific career.

◆ Your scores on the GRE. The next section provides some guidance on taking the GRE.

◆ Your participation in other activities. Were you involved in the psychology club? Did you participate in any research? Did you do any mentoring or volunteering? Did you participate in an internship?

◆ Your statement or essay. Usually you express your thoughts on why you want to pursue this degree and also explain what skills you have. Make sure to look at all activities and cast them as positives. For instance, if you were the events planner for your fraternity, include this experience, even if it's not directly a "psychology" activity. (In this case, focus on the skills: planning large events, maintaining a schedule, and so on.)

◆ Letters of recommendation. If you remember from Chapter 3, you were encouraged to network, volunteer, find a mentor, and get an internship. All of this work pays off when you can easily find relevant people who will write glowing letters of recommendation.

PREPARING FOR THE GRE

Try to take the GRE your junior year (one year before you graduate), but if you did not make the decision to go to graduate school until later, you may have to take this test your senior year.

For this test, you can find a variety of GRE preparations ranging from an expensive, intense study course to preparation books to sample examples. While you may not need the intense study course, you should look into some preparation work so that you know what to expect. What types of questions does the test include? What topics are covered? Check out books in your regular library, the career library at your school, or the bookstore. Also, check with your adviser; he or she may have resources for preparing for this exam.

GETTING LETTERS OF RECOMMENDATION

As mentioned, your college work should help you network and meet others who can write effective letters of recommendation. These letters are most effective when you know what the graduate committee is looking for in such a letter.

You might ask someone on the faculty with experience in writing letters of recommendation for a generic copy of a recommendation letter or a list of skills that professors think are critical. You can then review the letter or list, pursuing these skills and building up evidence of these same skills. You can also use the letter or list to relate existing experiences, skills, and knowledge to these essential grad school qualities.

PAYING FOR GRADUATE SCHOOL

When you continue your schooling, you need to pay for your additional education. Even if your parents provided help with your undergraduate degree, they are more likely to expect you to pay for any further studies.

You do have some avenues for pursuing financial help. First, you may apply for an assistantship. The role (and compensation) varies. For instance, you may become a teaching assistant and teach (or help teach) certain introductory psychology courses. You may help an instructor grade papers, prepare for class, and so on. You may do research. Check with the graduate department to apply for these opportunities. Often, an assistantship (or similar position) not only allows you to take a certain number of courses for free, but you may also receive a stipend and/or housing costs.

You can find other financial resources in work study; private, federal, and state loans (when you enter graduate school, you become a "professional student" and the cap on loan amounts changes); grants; fellowships; tuition-remission programs; and merit-based aid awarded on academic accomplishment, talent, or promise. You can find these resources through the university as well as possible outside sources.

Returning to School

You don't have to immediately go from undergraduate to graduate school. You may decide to pursue a career or a family. You may need a break from school. You can then return to graduate school later, when you feel ready.

In this case, you'll follow the same steps as someone who's applying as an undergraduate: You'll submit your transcripts and GPA, take the GRE, get letters of recommendation, and submit an application.

As a returning student, consider these tips:

◆ Renew any friendships or acquaintances you have from school. You might visit or write to faculty. You basically are looking for candidates for your letters of recommendation.

◆ Consider taking a few classes if you have been out of school for a while. This will help prepare you for returning to school. It may also refresh or remind you of some of the basic information you need to know.

◆ Decide how much help you need with the GRE. It's usually best to take this while in college when all the content you study is still fresh in your mind. If you have been out of school for a while, you may need to prepare more extensively for the GRE.

◆ When you write your essay or statement, account for your time away from school. Even if you were staying at home with a young child or working at a dead-end job, look at the skills and accomplishments you gained from these experiences. Staying home with a young child may have taught you time management. You may have connected and bonded with other parents and learned key coping skills. Try to present your experiences in a positive light that shows some connection or usefulness to the new path you are pursuing.

Chapter 5

Breaking into the Psychology Job Market

Times have changed; people no longer start and end their career with one company, retiring after 25+ years of service with that ubiquitous gold watch. In fact, the Bureau of Labor Statistics estimates that you'll have at least nine different jobs between college and retirement, but most researchers think this number is way too low. They estimate that you should plan on having 20 to maybe even 30 jobs. You can expect to not only change jobs, but also switch career fields entirely over the course of your working life. What else can you expect? Expect to be fired through no fault of your own. (Companies go out of business, merge, or downsize.) Expect to make some mistakes in your career. But that's jumping the gun. Let's take a step back and figure out how to get that job in the first place.

Planning Ahead

The things that can help you get a job once you graduate are, to start, following the suggestions in Chapter 3: participating in activities, working with a mentor, volunteering, investigating careers of interest *before* your last semester in college or graduate school, and participating in at least one internship. Students who have followed these guidelines are prepared and have a plan.

If you did not take advantage of these opportunities, you won't be on the same level as those with actual experience in psychology-related fields. One thing to keep in mind, though, is that employers and recruiters aren't looking for job hires based on major. Instead, they are looking at skills and characteristics. According to the National Association of Colleges and Employers, the top ten characteristics that employers look for in prospective hires include (in order of importance):

1. Communication skills

2. Honesty/integrity

3. Teamwork skills

4. Interpersonal skills

5. Motivation/initiative

6. Strong work ethic

7. Analytical skills

8. Flexibility/adaptability

9. Computer skills (basic knowledge of common office applications)

10. Self-confidence

That means if you have made the most of your college career, you should be sure to stress these qualities in addition to your psychology-related experiences, skills, and knowledge. If you didn't quite make the most of your opportunities during college, look for ways you did illustrate the preceding qualities. For instance, perhaps you were a cheerleader. You can use this experience to show how you work well with a team and to highlight your motivation skills. If you were president of your fraternity, you can use your experiences as a communicator, leader, and planner to show how that experience illustrated your mastery of these characteristics.

Preparing Your Resume

You can include the following characteristics in your resume, which you should prepare and have available. You'll need your resume for career fairs and actual job interviews. You can find entire books on creating a winning resume. This section summarizes some of the key points that are especially useful for finding jobs in psychology or a related field.

Consider these suggestions:

◆ Include all your pertinent contact information.

◆ Rather than list your career objective (the job you seek) at the top, begin with a strong selling point, a list of your key skills and experiences. Highlight your key knowledge, experiences, and characteristics. Summarize why someone should hire you. Succinctly include in a short list of what you have to offer.

◆ Highlight any psychology-related experience, including internships, mentoring, volunteer work, and so on. Don't just list the experience—for instance, "Volunteered for Suicide Hotline, September 2003 to September 2004." But go beyond the specifics of the title and dates and explain what you did. Show what skills you learned or practiced from this experience. "Learned how to communicate in stressful situations. Built trusting relationships based on my communication skills." And so on.

◆ Be sure to "sell" all your activities, not just those related directly to psychology. Think of how you spent your time during your college career and whether there's anything else worth mentioning.

◆ Include any and all relevant work experiences in addition to college. While some jobs may seem to have nothing to offer—such as if your first job was selling ice cream at the mall—perhaps the fact that you started working at 15 to pay for your private high school education makes mentioning that job worthwhile.

◆ When you think of job tasks, recast them in business terms. Also, if you are applying for a job in a psychology-related field, tie the job experience to that field specifically. For instance, suppose that you created a kiddie newsletter in your job as summer camp counselor; you could include the ability to create and publish appropriate, informative types of communication. This information will be useful if you are applying for a job in advertising.

◆ Use the resources at your career center to prepare your resume. The center is not only likely to have several books and examples in the library, but might also have career counselors who can critique and provide feedback on your resume.

You may also consider having business cards printed up with your name and contact information. These are easy to pass out, especially when networking.

Finding a Job

You've prepared your resume and are ready to go out and find a job. Here's the hardest part: Where do you start looking?

When most people think of finding a job, they think of the traditional methods: classified ads, and more recently, the Internet. But according to a recent article in *USA Weekend* about careers (Sept. 24–26, 2004), "more than 85% of all jobs are in a 'hidden job market' of unadvertised or created opportunities. That job market includes people hired from within the company and hired through word of mouth (without advertising the position)."

This section talks about some of the traditional job-hunting strategies. After all, you don't want to ignore the newspaper entirely; even if the listings don't include a job of interest to you, you can see what types of jobs are being advertised. You can also take a look at the Internet, although you'll soon realize that the Internet and its many job posting sites isn't the perfect solution. Finally, this section looks at some other, more promising, ways to look for available positions.

Published Job Openings

You can find published job openings in a number of places including your local newspaper, magazines, specific career magazines, and other places. The problem with published job openings is that once published, the competition for that opening becomes more intense. Still, if you see a job opening that sounds interesting, submit your resume.

One source of information about your local economy is your chamber of commerce. Check in with them for information about local companies, especially those that may be expanding or hiring.

WEB SITES

You can find a wealth of job-related sites on the Internet. Some provide job listings that you can search. Some provide job postings where you can post your resume; employers looking to fill positions can then search resumes and seek a match. Many provide career advice. Most provide a combination of these various services.

The best and most well known job site is monster.com. This site enables you to search for jobs, network with its other members, and get career advice. To search for jobs, you must sign up for a monster account.

In addition to this site, you may also try some of the following:

careerbuilder.com—This site claims "900,000 jobs, The Internet's Largest Job Search & Employment site." You can search for jobs, post resumes, get advice, find resources, and obtain information about career fairs. The problem with this site (as well as others like it) is that "psychology" isn't really a job category. To find psychology jobs, you have to browse through relevant categories or search for a particular job.

collegegrad.com—This site focuses on finding entry-level jobs and includes help for preparing resumes, cover letters, interviews, and more.

Try looking for sites that focus on a particular type of job. For instance, you can find online job clubs or career sites dedicated to a particular field; www.sciencejobs.com is one example.

If you want jobs specifically related to psychology, try www.psyccareers.com. The site functions like a typical job board: You post resumes and employers can then review the listings. You can also check out www.psychjobs.cjb.net (an index for psychology jobs and employment) and jobsinpsychology.com. To find more, search for "Psychology Jobs" on a search engine such as Google and see what sites turn up.

What can you gain from your Internet search? While you are hoping to find a job opening perfect for you, don't overlook the other information you can get from this search:

◆ What are the "hottest" jobs? What are the most advertised jobs?

◆ Read the advice at the various sites to see how you can improve your chances of getting a job. Ignore for the most part companies or advisers that make you pay for the advice.

◆ Look for companies or jobs of interest. While you may not get the job through the site postings, reading through the types of jobs that are available and the companies that are hiring can help you pinpoint the exact position you seek.

NETWORKING

If the want ads and Internet job sites don't work, what does? Networking. Most people find jobs through word of mouth, through networking, or through asking around.

Chapter 3 talks about beginning to build a network while in school. You should continue to do so in graduate school, during summer jobs, and while out of school. The more people included in your network, the better. Your network may include (but is not limited to):

◆ Family

◆ Friends

◆ Your family's friends

◆ Your friends' family

◆ Students

◆ Faculty

◆ Alumni

◆ Campus career center

◆ Former employers

◆ Former co-workers

◆ Customers or clients of former employers

◆ Competitors of former employers

◆ Neighbors

You can also network with any professionals you know or deal with, including your doctor, dentist, attorney, insurance agent, financial planner, hairdresser, barber, masseuse, personal trainer, coach, real estate broker, mechanic, veterinarian, bartender, child-care provider, and more.

Tell each of these individuals specifically (not hinting or hem-hawing around) that you are looking for a job. Give them a brief rundown on your education, your skills, and the type of job you want. Also, ask them to pass along your information to any other people who might be able to help.

CAREER CENTER, ON-CAMPUS RECRUITERS, AND CAREER FAIRS

In addition to publications and Web sites, your campus career center may sponsor career fairs or may host on-campus recruiters. (You can also find career fairs held through other sources, such as your local newspaper.) These are yet another possible source of job openings. Here's how to best take advantage of these events:

◆ Find out who's going to attend. If the fair, for instance, is geared toward the medical field, you may decide to take a close look at the types of workers they seek. If they are basically looking for nurses or anyone in the nursing field, you may consider skipping the fair.

◆ If the career fair is not limited to one area, take a look at the various companies that plan to attend. Are there any companies of interest to you? If so, make a list so that when you are at the fair, you can focus on these companies.

◆ Dress for an interview (at least a casual interview). Don't go in sweatpants and a T-shirt even if you think you are just browsing through. If someone wants to do an interview on the spot, you should be dressed for the part.

◆ Prepare a short statement (some people call this the "elevator speech"). This should sum up your education, experience, and career interest. Memorize it so that you get your main points across, but make sure when you "recite" it, you do so with enthusiasm and add pertinent facts and details based on the situation. You don't want your statement to sound canned.

◆ If you are asked what type of job you are seeking, be precise in explaining what you are looking for. If the company is not hiring in that area, ask the representative if they might know or recommend someone who is in your area or might be looking for someone with your skills. Ask them to keep you in mind.

◆ If you do participate in an interview (or several), be sure to ask how the process works. For instance, if they ask for your resume, does that mean they plan to call? Or are they just keeping it on file? If you do an initial interview, what's the next step? How should you follow up? When should you expect to hear from them? Don't walk away without knowing what is supposed to happen next.

FIND YOUR OWN JOB OPENINGS

Often you identify in your career search a particular company or organization that you want to work for. You can approach them directly to inquire about jobs. (You can also seek information interviews, as covered in Chapter 3, but remember when you conduct an information interview, you should never ask for a job.) You can check the company's Web page for openings or talk to human resources about current and upcoming positions.

Sometimes you'll take an entry-level position at a company just to get your start. Once you're hired, you'll gain the advantage of getting experience at the company. Plus, as mentioned, many jobs aren't advertised but are simply filled from within. Once you are "inside," you can keep alert to any possible new job positions and be first in line for consideration—sometimes even before the job has formally been posted.

Sometimes the job you want hasn't been created. And while you may have a hard time getting someone to listen to you so that you can sell them on the job, it can be done. This strategy works best if you are already working for the company. You can then spot the need for this job, create your job based on this need and your desires, and then "sell" the position to the company. You'll have more success if you show employers how the new job solves a problem, improves a situation, adds revenue, or provides some tangible benefit for the company or organization.

In trying to create your own job, look for economic, business, and demographic trends. For instance, the baby boomers are nearing retirement.

Around 77 million Americans will start hitting retirement age in 2010. What does that mean for you as a psychology major? What markets, jobs, or needs might these people have for someone with your skills? This population of people will need estate planning, mental health care dealing with aging, help with insurance programs, activity programs for seniors, and advocates for issues relating to their population, just to name a few needs. Consider what need you can fulfill by creating a specific job or by looking for an existing job in this market.

Interviewing for a Job

When you are asked for an interview, don't expect to put on your newly shined shoes and be ready. You have some preparation work to do. First, you need to research the company and organization. Second, you need to practice for the interview, anticipating the types of questions you'll be asked and preparing great responses. Third, you need to know how to follow up after the interview. This section discusses these skills.

Do Your Research

Before the interview, research the particular company or organization to find out more about it. What products do they make? What services do they offer? Who's the president of the company/organization? Is it a public or private company? How many people does the company employ? Where is the company headquarters located? You should know the answers to these and other key questions about the company or organization.

Where can you find the information? To start, visit the company or organization's Web site. Most companies include a page "about us" or something similar. They may talk about the company history, the mission statement, and so on. Look also for pages that describe how the company is organized as well as who holds key positions (note these names).

In addition, search the Internet for news stories about the company. Have they been in the news recently? If so, why? Are they launching a new product? Cutting back? Have they won any awards? Try to make sure you are up to date on any current news relating to the company.

You may also consider visiting sites that provide company overviews, such as Hoovers.com or Vault.com. These sites include profiles of thousands of companies and include more detailed research about the specific company. For the most part, you can look up general information about the company at these sites. For complete, detailed information, you may need to be a subscriber (pay a fee). Check with your school; it may have accounts with these types of sites. You may be able to get the detailed information going through your school's career center's connection.

As another source, if you know someone who works or has worked for that company, you may want to talk to that person. He or she may give you a better sense of the company atmosphere as well as what employers at the company look for in potential employees.

PRACTICE

In addition to doing your research, you should also prepare for the interview. In general, plan for five key points you want to make in the interview. Keep these points in mind; these are what you want the interviewer to remember about you. Also, be prepared to answer these typical questions:

♦ What do you know about our . . . (company, organization, etc.)? Here's where that research pays off!

♦ Tell me about yourself.

♦ What are your strengths/weaknesses?

♦ What would you like to change about yourself?

♦ Why did you leave your last job?

♦ Where do you see yourself five years from now?

♦ What are your goals?

♦ Why should I hire you?

In general, focus on what you can do for the company. Tell the interviewer what makes you unique as a person, what special skills you have, and what distinguishes you from the other people who want this same job. Stress the preparation work you have done (see Chapter 3) and the experiences and skills you already have for this position.

INTERVIEW TIPS

In addition to being prepared for the questions, keep in mind the following tips:

♦ **Dress appropriately.** If you've visited the company, perhaps on an information interview, you should get a sense of how employees dress. Know the night before what you're going to wear and make sure it's ready—no trying to find hosiery without a run in them or pants that aren't missing a button at the last minute.

♦ **Be on time.** No excuses.

♦ **Use a firm handshake and be sure to remember the person's name.** Say the person's name after you meet them ("It's great to meet you, Bob"); this can help you remember the name. If the interviewer has a card, you may ask for one. You can also provide your resume (and business card, if you have one).

♦ **When asking a question, be precise and to the point.** Don't blab on and on. Emphasize your strengths and show how your experience or education make you a good fit for the position.

♦ **Be friendly, but stick to professional issues.** Other topics such as an acquaintance you have in common or an upcoming event may pop up. That's fine, but keep your conversation focused on the job. Remember this is an interview, not a chat with a potential buddy.

THE INTERVIEW AND FOLLOW UP

At the end of the interview, usually the interviewer will ask, "Do you have any questions?" You should have some questions prepared, but don't just ask a question to ask a question. And above all else, don't ask, "Well, do I get the job?"

Instead, ask questions to learn more about the employer and company. For instance, you might ask how that person got his or her start. Ask for additional information about the position, what skills are needed and what resources are available. Also, try to get a sense of where the company is in the hiring process. Are there more people to interview? How soon will a decision be made? When would the new employee be asked to start work?

It's key that you know what to do next and how the overall interview process works. For instance, is this just an initial interview and should you expect to be invited back at least two more times to talk to the department head and then human resources before a hiring decision is made? You then at least have the framework for how the decision process happens.

Also, make sure you know what to do next. Should you call back? Will you be called? If so, by what date? If the company hasn't called by that date, ask whether it's okay if you follow up. Interviewing takes patience, but there's no sense waiting for a call if it's not going to come, so it's perfectly reasonable to ask whether you can call after a certain time limit to check on the job progress.

Be sure you send a handwritten thank-you note immediately after the interview. Little touches such as this make a difference; you might find handwritten notes antiquated in the age of email, but doing things "right" can make a big impression. Don't just say thank you in the note; restate your interest in the job as well as some of the reasons you think you are the perfect match for the position. (Even if you don't want the job after the interview, still send a thank-you note, but skip the parts about how you are a perfect match.)

If you don't get the job, try to learn more information about what you could have done differently. Don't be a pest about getting information, and don't demand information—the company does not owe you a long (or any!) explanation. But if you have a means to do so, learn whether the job was filled by someone else and what that person's qualifications were. (This is much easier to find out if you're already working in the company.) If no one was hired, was the position dropped? Use any information you gain during a follow-up to evaluate your interview skills. Did someone more qualified get the position? Not too much you can do about that except look for opportunities to increase your experience. Did someone you consider equal to you get the job? Perhaps he or she did a better job in the interview. What might you do better next time? Use each experience to better prepare you for your next chance. Also, be sure to ask the potential employer to pass along your resume to others looking to fill similar positions.

Chapter 6

Career Possibilities for a Psychology Major

Where can those with a major in psychology find work? In psychology, you'll find three basic kinds of jobs:

Clinical or counseling jobs

Research or computer-related jobs

Business or management jobs

Psychology majors work for businesses, corporations, non-profit organizations, educational institutions, and the government in a variety of jobs. They also work for themselves. According to the *Occupational Outlook Handbook,* common careers include counselor (a variety of types), educational and training manager, intelligence research specialist, labor relation specialist, market research analyst, personnel manager, probation officer, psychiatrist, psychologist, social worker, and others.

This chapter takes a look at the variety of career possibilities available to psychology majors, starting with the careers most commonly associated with a psychology degree. Many people do enter psychology with the goal of being some type of counselor or psychologist, and these are the types of jobs described first. The section explains the requirements (most of these careers require a master's or doctoral degree as well as certification), outlook, and salary range for this career path.

The chapter then looks at some other job possibilities. As mentioned, a degree in psychology provides you with versatile knowledge and skills that can be applied and used in a variety of careers. The second section picks out some other careers to consider with information about requirements and salary. Note that many of these jobs *do not* require advanced degrees.

Finally, because you truly can do so much with a degree in psychology (and this couldn't cover all the possibilities in detail), the last section describes how to investigate other jobs relating to psychology (or careers that require skills related to psychology studies). Here you can explore even more potential jobs as well as how and where to research to find out more detailed information.

Counselors and Psychologists

Many students enter college with the plan of getting a psychology degree and becoming a counselor or psychologist. What these students may not realize is that while these are perfect careers for psychology majors, they require additional schooling and usually certification. That information isn't meant to deter you from this type of career, but you will need to note the requirements as well as start thinking about what area you may potentially specialize in. This section starts with counseling careers and then covers careers as a psychologist.

COUNSELING CAREERS

Most counseling jobs require a master's degree as well as licensing requirements (specialized training, supervised hours, and certification exams). The exact requirements vary depending on type of counseling as well as your state's licensing procedures. Check with your graduate department as well as the state you plan to practice in to find out the specific requirements.

Within counseling, you may choose to specialize; some possibilities (described here) include addictions counselor, AIDS counselor, career counselor, clinical counselor, marriage and family counselor, mental health counselor, and rehabilitation counselor. The following list provides a brief description. Look at the table on p. 60 for salary information for each career.

◆ **Addictions Counselor.** In this type of counseling, you help people who are addicted to drugs and alcohol overcome these addictions. Your education and experience will help you understand what emotional and developmental issues cause addictive behavior and provide counseling to get your clients to understand these issues. As an addictions counselor, you also need to know about the physical effects of addiction and withdrawal. You can find more information about licensing and training at The National Association for Addiction Professionals, NAADAC Web site (www.naadac.org).

◆ **AIDS Counselor.** As an AIDS counselor, you have two areas of concern: prevention and treatment. On the prevention front, education is key. Your job is to let others (school children, health care workers, family members of someone with AIDS) know the dangers of HIV, how you can become exposed to HIV, and how to avoid HIV. In the treatment area, you work with infected patients and their loved ones. Some responsibilities include coordinating medical treatment; planning, making, and encouraging diet and lifestyle changes; coping with physical pain, fear, financial problems, and emotional stress; and many other things. For information and links to sites relating to AIDS, try the AIDS/HIV Disease and Medicaid Home Page (www.cms.hhs.gov/hiv/).

◆ **Career Counselor** (also known as Employment Counselor or Vocational Counselor). In this type of counseling, you help others with what you are doing now—assessing your skills, talents, and abilities; deciding on a career; developing skills to find a job (creating a resume, handling interviews, doing research, finding job openings); and ultimately applying for and receiving a job. For more information, visit the National Career Development Association Web site (www.ncda.org).

◆ **Clinical Counselor.** A clinical counselor is similar to a psychotherapist, but you may not have a doctorate and you may not follow Freudian-based theories in your practice. As a clinical counselor, you may want to work with certain types of issues including bereavement, learning disabilities, or post-traumatic stress. (Note that you don't have to specialize, and you may in fact prefer to work with a variety of clients and problems.)

Job	Median Salary	Lowest 10%	Middle 50%	Highest 10%
Addictions Counselor	$30,180	< 19,540	$24,350 – $37,520	> $45,570
AIDS Counselor	$40,540	< $24,770	$30,900 – $49,010	> $58,030
Career Counselor (a.k.a. Educational, Vocational, and School Counselors)	$44,100	< $24,930	$33,160 – $56,770	> $70,320
Clinical Counselor	$58,640	< $31,250	$40,400 – $69,250	> $88,930
Marriage and Family Counselor	$41,420	< $22,990	$29,460 – $48,180	> $62,390
Mental Health Counselor	$35,060	< $20,630	$25,260 – $42,170	>$54,650
Rehabilitation Counselor	$30,100	< $18,080	$21,720 – $35,650	>$47,100

* Based on 2002 and 2003 statistics from the Bureau of Labor Statistics

- ◆ **Marriage and Family Counselor.** Marriage and family counseling focuses on key family relationships: either between a couple (engaged, married, living together, and other situations) or within a family. Your role as counselor is to seek to improve the relationships by teaching and modeling good communication skills and constructive conflict management. The American Association for Marriage and Family Therapy Web site (www.aamft.org) contains helpful information.

- ◆ **Mental Health Counselor.** This type of counseling often overlaps and covers issues and problems mentioned in other types of counseling. For instance, as a mental health counselor, you may deal with addiction, depression, marriage, health problems, and more. You may treat people in individual or group settings. Visit the American Mental Health Counselors Association Web site for more information (www.amhca.org).

◆ **Rehabilitation Counselor.** In this type of counseling, you help people cope with the practical effects of disabling conditions, such as birth defects, illnesses, and injuries. Working with your clients, you help them handle or plan for independent living; teach them (or find resources for them to learn) vocational and social skills; and handle self-esteem, depression, and marriage and parenting issues. The National Rehabilitation Counseling Association Web site (www.nrca-net.org) can provide additional information.

In addition to the descriptions, you can look up the typical salaries for these careers. A good source for outlook and salary information is the Bureau of Labor and Statistics (www.bls.gov).

PSYCHOLOGIST CAREERS

Careers as psychologists, while commanding the highest salary in the psychology field, also require the most training. The exact requirements for certification and licensing vary depending on your state's licensing procedures. Check with your graduate department for information as well as the state you plan to practice in to find out the specific requirements.

The following lists some possible specialties you may consider as a psychologist along with a description of the specialty. Salary information is listed on p. 63. If you want to become a psychologist, you may consider the following areas of specialization:

◆ **Child Psychologist.** Child psychologists, as you might guess, focus their practice on children. You may treat children who are bereaved, traumatized, learning disabled, or depressed. If you choose this type of practice, you'll need to study child development as well as know how to treat these special conditions. As a child psychologist, you might work in a school, clinic, hospital, or private practice.

◆ **Clinical Psychologist.** If you become a clinical psychologist (the largest category of psychologists, by the way), you commonly work in counseling centers, independent or group practices, hospitals, or clinics. Clinical psychology covers a broad range of issues and problems. You may help mentally and emotionally disturbed clients adjust to life. You may work in rehabilitation centers, treating, for instance, patients with chronic pain or illness. You may help clients during times of personal crisis, such as divorce or the death of a loved one. As a clinical psychologist, it's common for you to give diagnostic tests and interview patients. You may provide individual, family, or group psychotherapy, and design and implement behavior modification programs. Other clinical psychologists work in universities and medical schools, where they train graduate students. Some administer community mental health programs.

Note that, except for in New Mexico, clinical psychologists generally are not permitted to prescribe medications to treat patients; only psychiatrists and other medical doctors may prescribe medications. These restrictions might change in the future on a state-by-state basis.

- ◆ **College Professor.** You may decide you love psychology so much that you want to teach it to others. In that case, you may consider a career as a professor of psychology. In addition to teaching psychology courses, you most likely will be required to continue your education by publishing or conducting psychological research.

- ◆ **Counseling Psychologist.** Counseling psychologists use various techniques, including interviewing and testing, to advise people on how to deal with problems of everyday living. They work in settings such as university counseling centers, hospitals, and individual or group practices.

- ◆ **Developmental Psychologist.** This type of psychologist seeks to understand the physiological, cognitive, and social development that takes place throughout life. In practice, they may specialize in a particular phase of development (infant, childhood, adolescence, maturity, old age) and handle any problems or changes associated with that phase. As another option, you may want to study developmental disabilities and their effects. For instance, research is increasingly developing ways to help elderly people remain independent as long as possible.

- ◆ **Experimental Psychologist.** If you are interested in this type of psychology, you're most likely fascinated by behavior processes and enjoy conducting experiments using human beings and animals, such as rats, monkeys, and pigeons. Prominent areas of study in experimental research include motivation, thought, attention, learning and memory, sensory and perceptual processes, effects of substance abuse, and genetic and neurological factors affecting behavior. If you work in this area, you commonly work in university and private research centers and in business, non-profit, and governmental organizations.

◆ **Industrial/Organizational Psychologist.** This type of psychologist concerns him or herself with the workplace and seeks to improve productivity and the quality of work life. If you pursue this type of psychology, you also will most likely be involved in research on management and marketing problems. If you work for a particular company, you may conduct applicant screening, training and development, counseling, and organizational development and analysis. You might also be hired as a consultant to offer solutions or recommendations for a particular problem or set of problems.

Job	Median Salary	Lowest 10%	Middle 50%	Highest 10%
Child Psychologist	$51,170	<$30,090	$38,560 – $66,970	>$87,060
Clinical and Counseling Psychologists	$51,000	<$30,000	$36,700 – $67,000	>$87,000
College Professor (4-year college)	$68,180	<$30,420	$41,340 – $72,000	>$94,730
Developmental Psychologist	$50,000	<$30,000	$36,000 – $65,000	>$86,000
Experimental Psychologist	$50,000	<$30,000	$36,000 – $65,000	>$86,000
Industrial and Organizational Psychologists	$63,700	<$36,600	$48,500 – $81,900	>$112,700
Neuropsychologist	$51,140	<$30,000	$37,500 – $67,000	>$87,000
Psychotherapist	$51,170	<$30,090	$38,560 – $66,970	>$87,060
Social Psychologist	$51,000	<$30,000	$36,700 – $67,000	>$87,000

* Based on 2002 and 2003 statistics from the Bureau of Labor Statistics

- **Neuropsychologist.** A clinical neuropsychologist studies, diagnoses, and treats human behavior as it relates to normal and abnormal functioning of the central nervous system.

- **Psychotherapist.** Psychotherapy focuses on treating mental and emotional disorders through psychological methods based on Sigmund Freud's theories. This type of therapist does not use drug therapy or electroconvulsive therapy, although the psychotherapy may be combined with medical approaches like these.

- **Social Psychologist.** If you want to learn more and improve the way people interact with others and with their social environment, you may consider becoming a social psychologist. This type of psychologist usually works in organizational consultation, marketing research, systems design, or other applied psychology fields. Prominent areas of study include group behavior, leadership, attitudes, and perception.

More Psychology Major Career Possibilities

As mentioned, some students do pursue a psychology major with the intent of getting a master's or doctoral degree to work as a counselor or psychologist. But many students do not, and a psychology degree is applicable to many, many professions outside the counseling/psychologist field. This section briefly highlights some careers for your consideration. (Keep in mind that this list is by no means comprehensive.)

ADVERTISING (MEDIA BUYER)

A media buyer negotiates, schedules, and buys advertising space in the appropriate media. With a college degree in psychology, you can help identify the target audience, ensuring your advertising campaign reaches the right people. You also work to negotiate the best prices for the ad space. As a media buyer, you work with a media planner (see the following section) to carry out your plan. A bachelor's degree is usually enough to get you started in the field, because only limited experience is needed at first, and you will have a supervisor to help you along. The starting salary in a large city can be $40,000 to $53,000 per year.

ADVERTISING (MEDIA PLANNER)

A media planner researches and develops media plans. Your psychology degree again helps you to identify a target audience and the best way of reaching it, as well as to successfully recommend the right kind and amount of advertising for your clients' budget and goals. You can usually get started in advertising (since you work with a supervisor at first) with a bachelor's degree. The starting salary in a large city can be $44,000 to $56,000 per year.

CHILD WELFARE CASEWORKER

A caseworker oversees the progress of children who are at risk due to abuse, neglect, and other traumatic family situations. Your psychological skills help you conduct interviews and make decisions about the right course of action for the children and their families. Although many caseworkers have social work degrees, a psychology degree is also acceptable in many places; the two fields overlap quite a bit, and you may be planning to go back for a graduate degree later on. Starting salaries can be in the $40,000-per-year range, although many state and local budgets have not been able to guarantee this rate.

EMPLOYMENT COUNSELOR (AT A COLLEGE)

As an employment counselor at a college, you help students find jobs—whether full-time after graduation, part-time during the school year, or during school breaks. To promote job opportunities, you likely invite employers to campus for job fairs, interviews, and general recruiting. To help with career planning, you can use tests, such as the Myers-Briggs test, to help students find jobs that suit their interests and personality. You may also run resume writing workshops and mock interviews. You also post job opportunities and maintain an alumni network so that students can find people to answer their questions about particular careers. This aspect also requires putting psychology into practice, so you can negotiate between students, alumni, and employers, and encourage their participation in your office's activities. Your bachelor's degree may be enough to get you hired; you'll be assisting more-senior counselors at first, which will give you valuable on-the-job training. Salaries may be in the range of $39,000 to $49,000 per year. If you decide to get additional schooling, you may become a licensed career counselor (see the preceding section that talks about this career).

Hotel Manager

To manage the overall daily operations of a hotel/motel, you need your psychological training so that you can supervise and direct your staff and sense and respond to the needs of your guests. Starting pay can be $28,000 to $34,000 per year.

Human Resources Specialist

Depending on your company's needs, you create and carry out human resources programs and policies including staffing, compensation, benefits, visa/green-card processing, employee relations, training, and health and safety programs. Your training in psychology should help you assess job candidates and employees who are up for promotion, as well as to sense and respond to any problems that develop. Companies vary in their educational requirements; some will accept a bachelor's degree, while others will want you to go on for graduate work. Salaries start at $41,000 to $51,000 per year.

Insurance Agent

As an insurance agent, you sell insurance plans to new and current clients. A psychology major is a good fit for this job because you should be able to discuss sensitive matters relating to health, mortality, and property loss, especially when dealing with clients who are already in distress. Licensing varies by state, although as a new employee, you may be able to operate under your supervisor's license, and many firms offer training programs. Starting salaries can be $40,000 to $50,000 per year, but some companies pay agents on commission.

Market Research Analyst

As a psychology major, you learn a lot about research techniques, statistics, reports, and other research skills. This makes you a perfect fit for many types of jobs that require research, including a market research analyst. In this job, you gather and analyze data to evaluate the needs and reactions of consumers for existing and potential products and services. You need to be sensitive to market conditions and changes in the industry that may affect sales. Because you have studied psychology, you are good at recognizing how people in your target audience feel, and you can communicate their reactions to your clients, who will better understand what changes are needed in their products and services. Salaries can start at $41,000 to $53,000 per year.

POLICE OFFICER

As a new police officer, you usually start as a patrol officer, protecting your assigned area to prevent and discover crime and to enforce regulations. Although your psychology degree is not a requirement, it will help you in conducting investigations, making arrests, and testifying in court, as well as responding to calls and taking necessary action at the scene of a crime or disturbance. Promotions within the department are merit-based, so you may not need any further degrees. Be prepared for adrenaline highs and lows; at times, you may face physical danger, but you'll also spend a lot of time doing paperwork. Police departments offer training through police academies to candidates who pass a qualifying exam. Patrol officers earn $41,000 to $53,000 per year.

PSYCHOLOGY PARAPROFESSIONAL

Although you are not a licensed psychologist, you can help evaluate patients for mental, emotional, or behavioral disorders and offer preliminary diagnoses for your supervisors to follow up on. You may even offer limited treatment, using talk therapy in individual or group settings, although you cannot prescribe medication. Paraprofessionals help take the burden off overworked licensed psychologists in settings with heavy caseloads, such as public hospitals. Salaries vary widely by location and setting.

PUBLIC RELATIONS SPECIALIST

As a public relations specialist, you prepare and distribute information about your clients to the media, often in the form of press releases. Your major in psychology helps you tailor your approach to get the best results, both in terms of the wording of your press releases and in convincing your media contacts to use them. Salaries may start at $38,000 to $48,000 per year.

RETAIL BUYER

In this career, you negotiate the purchasing of materials, equipment, and supplies from vendors, determining the best suppliers. Psychology prepares you for negotiating; as a retail buyer, you may be able to talk vendors into offering a better price. Entry-level pay is $25,000 to $37,000 per year.

RETAIL STORE MANAGER

As a retail store manager, you manage the daily operation of a retail store, including customer service, sales, and inventory control. You may have to keep financial records, although your store may employ someone else for that responsibility. Your knowledge of psychology helps you to implement and update store policies and procedures, supervise staff, and deal with customer requests and complaints. One downside, however, is that you may be required to work nights and weekends. Salaries start at $40,000 to $52,000 per year.

TEACHER

As an elementary or secondary school teacher, you prepare lesson plans and instruct children or adolescents and evaluate their performance. Your knowledge of psychology will help you better understand your students' needs and enable you to encourage them in their studies. Plus, you should be skilled at managing the class as a whole. Most states require that teachers become certified and eventually earn a master's degree, but requirements vary so much from place to place and from one year to the next that you should check to see what they are in your area. Still, a bachelor's degree may be enough to start with; many schools and districts will help you obtain the graduate work or other training you'll need for certification.

For a high school job, you may also need to have some knowledge and experience in the particular subject(s) you will be teaching; this can be a natural if you took a double major or are fully bilingual, for example. Big-city salaries can begin at $40,000 per year.

Teachers' aides, who help the classroom teacher prepare and teach lessons and evaluate students' progress, do not face the same certification

Top Jobs for Women

What are the top-paying professions for women with an undergraduate degree according to a recent "On the Job" column in *All Woman* (Fall 2004)? The following shows the annual salary in thousands (K):

Pharmacist	74.9K
Computer Software Engineer	73.2K
Computer Programmer	60.1K
Financial Services Sales Agent	59.7K
Personal Financial Adviser	57.7K
Market Research Analyst	53.4K
Registered Nurse	46.7K
Accountant	45.4K
Writer	42.5K
Public Relations Specialist	41.0K

requirements (although a background check is usually required). Salaries for teacher aides are $19,000 to $23,000 per year.

Still More Career Possibilities

This chapter just touches on some of the many career possibilities for a student with a degree in psychology (bachelor's, master's, and doctoral). But don't be limited to these suggestions. Think about your skills. Remember, as mentioned in Chapter 5, employers aren't looking for the content knowledge, but the skills and characteristics you have (honesty, computer skills, initiative, and so on).

This section provides a list of some other job ideas to consider. You'll also learn how to find out more about these (or any jobs) as well as where to look for other jobs recommended for psychology majors.

JOBS FOR PSYCHOLOGY MAJORS

Most colleges provide a list or information on their Web site with examples of the types of careers applicable to a major in psychology. For instance, Rutgers lists the jobs of its psychology graduates as well as psychology alumni (careerservices.rutgers.edu/Mpsychology.html). The University of Texas Web site (www.utexas.edu/student/careercenter/careers) is another site that lists applicable careers for specific majors.

You can find other similar lists at the following:

♦ University of North Carolina's "What Can I Do With A Major In...?" (www.uncw.edu/stuaff/career/majors)

♦ University of Kansas Academic Majors Career Resources (www.ukans.edu/~uces/major/index/shtml)

♦ Florida State University's Match Major Sheets (career.fsu.edu/ccis/matchmajor/matchmenu.html)

♦ University of Tennessee's "What can I do with this major?" career.utk.edu/students/majors.asp)

This last site is incredibly helpful; it provides links to a PDF table that lists career areas, typical (possible) employees, and strategies for getting a job in that area.

RESEARCHING CAREER PARTICULARS

If you find a career of interest and want to find more detailed information (a job description, salary range, work environment, requirements, likely employers, professional associations, and other useful information), you can use any number of resources to locate this information. Some popular resources include:

♦ The *Occupational Outlook Handbook* (hardcopy in library) or online at www.bls.gov/oco.

♦ O*NET, which includes more comprehensive information (online. onetcenter.org)

Chapter 7

Case Studies

The best way to learn about how to find a job and the various types of ways you can use a psychology degree is to listen to and read about real stories, real people, and real experiences. That's the focus of this chapter: case studies that focus on several different individuals. From each story, you can see how that person found his or her job and what he or she likes about it, as well as tips on how to succeed. From these case studies, you should gain insight into the many possibilities of a psychology major as well as how to plan the steps in your own educational and career quest.

You'll read about a variety of people with a variety of jobs from an art therapist to a school psychologist to a forensic psychologist. While the careers and career paths vary, they all have one thing in common: They majored in psychology.

Beth, Art Therapist

When I was a child, I was a skilled artist and loved painting and working on artistic projects. My friends expected me to become an artist, but I didn't plan to pursue this type of career. When I started college I picked psychology as a major because it was interesting to me. At the same time, I still took art courses. One day it dawned on me that when I was under stress, I turned to drawing as a release. I thought, "If it worked for me, imagine how I could use art to help people who had much bigger problems than everyday stress!" I realized that I could combine both of my passions: art and psychology. I began to think about becoming an art therapist.

WHAT I DO

As an art therapist, I work at an outpatient clinic at a hospital. I provide psychological therapy to people by helping them create artwork. Many of my patients have trouble communicating with normal speech, and the art allows them to express themselves without words. Some of my patients are children who have been through traumatic experiences, such as crimes or disasters, but are so young that they don't have the vocabulary to talk about it in regular therapy. It's easier for them to draw pictures about how they're feeling or to take out their anger on a piece of clay.

Other people are mentally disabled, and even if they haven't been through trauma, they can benefit from art therapy to help them develop life skills. For example, verbally teaching some disabled people how to set the table for dinner can be difficult, but if we draw pictures of a set table or build a model of one, they can grasp how to do it. In this way, some disabled people can learn to live more independently and even get a job!

Some people have lost some or all of their speaking ability because of an injury or a stroke. Other departments in the hospital may be working with them to regain the ability to talk, but in the meantime, my job is to help these patients with the psychological distress that this condition has caused. Art is both a creative outlet for their feelings and a way that they can communicate while they're recovering from their injury, such as a broken jaw or paralysis.

WHY I MAJORED IN PSYCHOLOGY

People who knew me back in high school thought of me as the artistic kid. I had always been the type to doodle in my notebooks, and in high school I found some practical uses for my artistic skills. Because I could draw well, I became the "go-to" girl for everything from illustrating the school newspaper to designing scenery for the spring play. I made my own greeting cards and even made a senior class logo for T-shirts. Not only was it a great ego boost to have my classmates and teachers ask me to take charge of all these artistic projects, but I also loved seeing how my art could make such a big difference when I used it to cheer up a sick friend with a card or to turn an empty stage into the setting of a play.

I began to think about a psychology major the summer before eleventh grade. Most of my friends expected me to become an artist, and at camp that summer the girls were looking through my sketchbook and asked me if I was planning to be an artist. I said no, explaining that I thought it would be too hard to earn a living that way. While I loved art, I didn't think I could earn a living as an artist. I didn't fancy the idea of being a "starving artist" living in a garret somewhere. And commercial art (which is more lucrative) didn't interest me. Naturally, someone then asked what I *did* want to do for a living, and I mentioned that I was interested in psychology.

I was always drawn to psychology, as I realized that I had become more aware of psychology just from drawing pictures of people I knew. The process of getting someone's facial expression down on paper made me more curious about them and what, as they say, made them "tick." I figured I might like some kind of psychology as a profession, and I could keep art as a hobby—psychology as my vocation and art as my avocation.

One of the girls in our camp career discussion suggested that I could be an art therapist. At the time, I said no! I was afraid that if art became part of my career, it would become a work obligation and I wouldn't be able to enjoy it in my free time anymore. But by the time I was halfway through college, I realized that this career was a perfect combination for me.

How My Psychology Major Prepared Me for My Job

My psychology major helped prepare me for my job because I learned about typical topics covered in a psychology major: how people develop psychologically during their life span, how people learn, and how people react emotionally to traumatic events in their lives. I also learned about abnormal psychology, and, of course, the different types of therapy. That knowledge helps me evaluate the people I treat. I know how their behavior compares to the norm, and I have an idea of what might help them.

At the same time I was studying psychology, I was also taking art courses. I noted how art personally helped me relieve stress and let go of whatever was bothering me. I thought about how art might play the same role in other's lives with even bigger problems. This was confirmed in my art history class when I learned about van Gogh's mental illness. I realized then that I was already melding the two areas.

How I Got Started in a Career in Art Therapy

When I really got interested in art therapy, I spoke to my major adviser, who was also one of my professors. She suggested that I try an internship where I could observe real practitioners in action, and she helped me find a position in the clinic at my university's hospital. One morning and one afternoon a week (which was how I could fit it around my class schedule), I would go over to the clinic and assist the therapists.

One of the things I helped with was bringing art therapy to the children's wards. When kids were too sick or injured to come to the clinic, we'd bring a cart full of art supplies to them in their beds and draw together and talk about how the kids felt. One little boy who had broken both legs in an accident started off drawing depressing pictures of mangled stick figures being injured the way he was, and I asked him to explain what he drew. He described the accident, and we talked about how people could make things safer so that other kids wouldn't get hurt the way he did. Gradually, his drawings became more hopeful. He drew little stick figures that were shown helping each other and protecting one another from danger. I was so excited when I realized how much progress he had made just from our sessions. I knew this was the kind of work I wanted to do.

What Other Education, Training, and Experiences I Pursued

After college, I started a master's degree in art therapy at a state university. The advantage of a state university is that it provides opportunities to work in state programs. I was matched with a prison program, of all things, and I worked with emotionally disturbed convicts. Some of them had mental deficiencies—low IQ, for instance—and regular talk therapy was beyond their conversational ability. Others had such violent tempers that they couldn't settle down enough for talk therapy. Doing artwork with a therapist was calming for many of them, and it let them express themselves in ways that their vocabularies or tempers would not.

In the prison program, I also started to see other kinds of art being used for therapy. Drawing was the norm at the hospital, because it's relatively clean and can even be done while sitting up in bed, but in the prison program, we also used paints and clay and other messier materials.

Seeing people express themselves in a three-dimensional medium was interesting.

I have to admit, though, the prison program frightened me. I was working with convicted criminals, including some violent offenders, and I'm a short woman with no self-defense training. Working with this population was so educational for me, but I didn't want to be afraid to go to work every day!

The master's program helped me fulfill my state's requirements for certification and licensing. The coursework and supervised fieldwork at school got me registered with the Art Therapy Credentials Board. I took the exam and became board certified. The Board requires me to keep up with developments in the field by taking continuing education courses. This requirement is not that difficult because I have access to a lot of universities near where I live, so it's easy to find one. I can also fulfill this requirement by attending certain professional conferences, which are often at nice resorts in interesting places around the country!

WHAT HELPED ME SUCCEED

Some key things helped me become successful. These include the following:

◆ I think I found my "perfect" career so quickly because I had the advantage of knowing about this career at an early age. Even though I wasn't sure it was what I wanted to do at first, I had the idea in the back of my mind. Not everyone is aware of a specific career possibility at such a young age, so I know I got lucky. You should learn about the various job opportunities as much as you can. (This book is a great start in that direction!)

◆ My adviser in college was a big help; taking the time to discuss my interests with her was a smart move. When she understood where my interests lay, she was better equipped than I was to steer me in the right direction.

◆ That first internship at the university hospital was also a great step for me. Not only did I get to see what art therapists do and what effects the therapy can have, but I also got to try working with some of the patients. Before my adviser recommended this internship, I didn't realize that this kind of opportunity was open to undergraduates who hadn't yet committed to the profession, or that I would actually be allowed to work with actual patients!

◆ Another helpful move was attending some of those professional conferences. Even while I was still in college, I went to a couple of them in my city. They offered reduced rates for students and even had a couple of workshops to help people entering the career. Conferences are also a good place to meet people in the field and learn more about the different ways people work in this profession.

PITFALLS TO AVOID

As for pitfalls, I did encounter one, but it wasn't a professional problem—more of a personal one. When I took the prison internship, I had misgivings, and even though I learned a lot, I was uncomfortable working there. But I was afraid that if I said anything, my supervisors would think I was unprofessional, immature, or even politically incorrect. I think I could have been more assertive and asked for a placement that suited me better.

It's not a moral judgment, but if you're not comfortable in your work environment, you're not going to be a very effective therapist. There are so many populations an art therapist can work with, and you have to find a setting you like. Students going into this field should really take the time to research their options.

Also, make sure you keep up with licensing requirements. An accredited graduate-school program will help you do that, but I know I was thrown for a loop when one of the state requirements was changed while I was still a student. It meant I had to take a particular class the next semester, so it's a good thing I knew about it in time!

WHAT I LOVE ABOUT MY JOB

This job combines two of my favorite disciplines—art and psychology. I'm very lucky and very happy to be doing the things I love. In this career, I can use these things I love to help people overcome serious problems. Even if I can't make the problems go away, I can help my clients learn to cope with them or even work around them in a healthy, productive way. And because I work with visual media, I can really see tangible results of the progress we make together. That's really satisfying!

THINGS ON THE JOB I COULD DO WITHOUT

This is easy: paperwork! Between insurance forms, progress reports, and record keeping for both the hospital and the clinic, paperwork can feel like a full-time job. I'm just glad there's a clerical staff to handle the financial paperwork, but I have to handle the rest of it myself.

Also, I do find some cases are upsetting. Although I'm glad when I can make cancer patients feel better, for example, it's so sad to know that ultimately, some of them die, and I can't save them. In cases like that, I like to give some of their artwork to their grieving families if I think it will help them to have happy memories. Also, some of my patients are crime victims, and even if I can help them, I get so angry at the things that were done to them, especially if the person who hurt them hasn't been brought to justice.

MY WORK SCHEDULE AND LIFESTYLE

One of the great things about the setting I'm working in is the regular hours. Because the clinic is attached to a hospital, I'm well aware that some of my colleagues in the main building have to work night shifts and weekends, or they get called in for emergencies in the middle of the night. Even the psychologists who work in the main part of the hospital as opposed to the clinic have to take their turn being on call at all hours.

The work schedule was one of the things I thought about when I was first starting out because I knew that I wanted to get married and have children some day. In my department, the therapists can arrange their hours to suit their family life. They can leave early to pick their kids up from school, or work limited days and hours when they have babies at home, or even schedule their appointments around graduate school and continuing education classes. I really appreciate that flexibility.

Also, working at a hospital clinic means good health-care benefits and other perks. The salary isn't as high as it might be in a fancy private practice, but it's reasonable, and I don't have to worry about finding new patients and promoting my services. It's true that I have to put up with hospital rules and regulations, but for me, it's worth it because it allows me to devote more time to my personal life.

Most days, I work a regular eight-hour day, although I sometimes get a long stretch of free time in the afternoon when no appointments are scheduled. As long as someone else on staff is available, I can leave the clinic and run errands, go see a museum or gallery exhibit, or even work out at the hospital gym. When there's a professional conference in town that I want to go to, I can reschedule my appointments around it, and my department picks up the cost for registration fees (and travel to out-of-town conferences); the hospital wants to encourage professional development. I've even taken art classes during the workday, and I was able to arrange my work schedule around the class.

Occasionally, I do special work outside the office. For example, after September 11, 2001, a friend who teaches at an elementary school asked me to come and lead the class in an art-therapy project. I helped the kids make a memorial quilt; each student made one square of the quilt. After it was displayed on the wall in the school, the class donated it to a local firehouse. The children were able to use the project to express feelings that they couldn't quite put into words, from their fear and grief to their gratitude to the heroes who rushed to the scene. The firefighters loved it, too. Some of those big, tough guys were moved to tears, and they all appreciated the recognition from the school kids.

Art therapy is a good career for someone who is patient and understanding, who loves art, who can deal with people who are ill or handicapped or impaired in some other way, and who enjoys a lot of hands-on work.

Statistics About This Job

Starting salaries for art therapists are about $25,000; the median salary is about $33,000. Art therapists in private practice can earn $75 to $90 an hour for individual sessions.

Alex, Sports Psychologist

In sports, there's a great emphasis placed on winning, and teams have turned to using sports psychologists to gain an edge in understanding motivation, to overcome mental obstacles or fears, and to recover from injuries and setbacks. That's what I do; I am a sports psychologist.

I didn't have a set game plan when I started college. The school I attended had an excellent psychology department, and I took one class and then another and then another and ended up majoring in psychology with a special interest in issues of self-esteem and motivation. I'm not a great athlete, but I am a fan, and when I heard during the broad-cast of a football game that a player needed to see a good "sports psy-chologist" to get back on track, it struck me as a great career match for me, especially since my main area of interest within psychology was self-esteem and motivation.

What I Do

I'm a sports psychologist for a professional baseball team. In this job, I work with athletes on different psychological issues. For instance, I help them to improve their motivation, I help them set achievement goals, and I help them conquer those mental demons that can hold them back. I also work with players who have been injured or have not been playing well to mentally overcome the injury or setback.

In addition to working with the players, I also work with the coach-ing staff. My main goal is to tailor the training program for the best psychological approach. I help the staff understand the needs and moti-vations of the players so that they understand the best way to coach the individual as well as the team as a whole.

Why I Majored in Psychology

I didn't know what I wanted to major in when I started college, but I took an introduction to psychology course to fulfill a general freshman requirement, and the professor was great. I had to take a lab course for college, too, and I'm really not a big science guy, so when I saw that the same professor was teaching a psych lab the next semester, I signed up. I didn't have a particular career goal, but one psychology course just led to another, and before I knew it, I was a psychology major!

How My Psychology Major Prepared Me for My Job

Within my psychology major, I became especially interested in the area of self-esteem and motivation. At first, it reminded me of applying to college. I remember some of my high school classmates talking about the reasons why they would or wouldn't apply to a particular college, and when I took psychology in college, I thought about how much self-esteem played a role in these decisions.

One day in my senior year, I was watching a game on TV with my friends in the dorm, and the commentators were discussing one of the players, who they felt was having a motivation problem after losing out in the contract negotiations. One of them mentioned that this athlete would have to put in some time working with the team psychologist, and it's like a light bulb went on for me! I'm not a great athlete myself, but I am a fan, and sports psychology struck me as a great career for someone whose studies and interests are specifically centered on self-esteem and motivation.

To learn more about the field, I actually looked up the offices of a local professional sports team and called to ask if they had a psychologist on staff who would speak with me. A little psychology helped me get through to the right people and convince them that I wasn't just some crazy fan! The team psychologist was really great. He answered my questions and let me come down and see where he worked and what he did. I even got a couple of autographs in the process. But more importantly, the guy became an unofficial mentor to me, and he gave me a lot of helpful tips about getting into the business.

WHAT OTHER EDUCATION, TRAINING, AND EXPERIENCES I PURSUED

After college, I went to a graduate school that had a sports psychology specialty, although it wasn't a separate degree from general psychological counseling. The specialty dictated taking relevant classes, such as a thesis-level seminar on sports psychology and supervised training off campus with experienced professionals. I also took some cross-registration courses at another division of my university to learn more about the physiology involved in sports and sports medicine so that I would understand more when dealing with injured athletes.

The most important thing required for certification as a sports psychologist is supervised fieldwork. A whole list of accepted and unaccepted job descriptions can be counted for this requirement. I did my fieldwork at two local high schools, working with the varsity coaches to help encourage the kids, and also working with college guidance counselors to help seniors who were applying to college on athletic scholarships. It was an interesting experience, because I was working with kids only a few years younger than I was, and it took me back to that whole world of teenagers' concerns. The students would come to me for advice about all kinds of non-sports issues, like their social lives or their families, and it really gave me a chance to stretch my skills. I didn't know it at the time, but this experience would come in handy when I started working with professional athletes!

WHAT HELPED ME SUCCEED

I think a couple of things helped me succeed in getting to where I am in my career as a sports psychologist. While these pertain to my career, I think they would be helpful and adaptable to most fields in psychology. Here are some of the things that I think gave me an advantage:

- ◆ Contacting an actual sports psychologist. I'm still proud of myself for contacting that local team's psychologist. The man was very helpful to me, and if I hadn't had the idea of calling the team office, I wouldn't have had the chance to learn from him. It's difficult to make contacts, to reach out to those who are in positions where you want to be. But most people are happy and honored to help. And if not, try the next person. Mentoring can be so key to not only learning about careers, but also making connections in that career.

- ◆ Another smart move was that I noticed while reading some American Psychological Association literature that they have a division on sports psychology; this division offers memberships to college students. I joined and took advantage of this membership so that I could learn more about the specialty. I also received their newsletter, which kept me up to date on happenings in that field, and I attended a conference. The division has mentoring and other resources for students who are interested in becoming sports psychologists. Check out the APA literature and, if possible, join and participate in the division(s) that interest you.

PITFALLS TO AVOID

The only problem I had with my career choice was that no one really knew much about this particular specialty at my undergraduate school (as great as my school's psych program is). That's why I had to take the initiative and find a real sports psychologist to answer my questions. I liked my college, and I'm not sorry I went there, but if I had known back in high school that I would become interested in sports psychology, I might have applied specifically to colleges with programs in this area. Things ended up working out, and it's difficult to know exactly what you want to do when you start college, so while it would have been nice to attend a college that had sports psych programs, I still ended up where I wanted to be.

WHAT I LOVE ABOUT MY JOB

I love being on the inside in the world of professional sports. I may not be one of the jocks myself, but I'm a big fan, and I have a job where the athletes come to me and talk about personal matters (very much like in my training fieldwork when high school students confided in me). The athletes look to me for advice, and they treat me with great respect, even though they're the celebrities. It's very cool. And when I watch a game and see one of the players I worked with make that winning play, it's a great feeling to know that my input helped him get there.

One of the perks of my job is that I get to see the games, and I can even get tickets for guests. I love the idea of bringing my kids to games in a few years. I'll probably be the most popular dad on the block! I also get to do some traveling, which I like to a certain degree. I get to meet all kinds of people, including celebrities, and I attend parties and other special events.

THINGS ON THE JOB I COULD DO WITHOUT

Gossip is a big problem. Not that I gossip—it's unethical—but I do know a lot of personal information about some well-known athletes. I've even had some tabloid reporters call the office and offer to pay me for some inside scoop, as if I'd be stupid enough to jeopardize my career that way! Sometimes I have to work hard to reassure some of the players that I won't tell their secrets. I guess all therapists have to build a good rapport with their clients, but my clients are in the public eye, so it's particularly important. And it is hard, sometimes, to keep a straight face when I'm not at work and I hear or read something about an athlete that I know isn't true!

I also have trouble with athletes who do dumb things and get into trouble with the law. I understand that they're under a lot of pressure, but I'm there to help with that, so I hate when they throw away my advice and possibly their careers getting high or assaulting someone. Then when the team makes them come see me, they're angry and resentful. It's easier for me to be understanding when they just have performance anxiety or something they didn't bring on themselves. But part of the job is dealing with these situations in a professional manner. I think I'm getting better with practice.

Another thing that is more of a problem lately is the travel. I enjoy visiting new places, but I'm a dad now, so it's harder to just take off and leave my family at home. Most of the trips are planned in advance, so we're ready for it, and I can sometimes bring the family along. But there are emergency trips sometimes, like if one of the guys on my team is injured or gets into some other trouble at an away game. I've occasionally had to fly out to some other city—sometimes in the middle of the night because of time zones—on almost no notice. It doesn't happen a lot, and my wife does understand, but it's a burden on her when I'm not there to do my share of the parenting.

MY WORK SCHEDULE AND LIFESTYLE

For my work schedule, I hold regularly scheduled appointments usually during the day. I meet with individual athletes who need to see me privately when they get a break from practice (or during practice, if the player is on the disabled list). I also meet with the coaches to discuss motivational training techniques and any concerns they have about athletes who are having problems. When the team is considering acquiring a new player or renewing someone's contract, they like to get my input on the guy's personality: Does he fit in with the rest of the team? Does he have an attitude problem or personal issues that might hinder his performance?

If someone gets injured, I go see him in the hospital if necessary. I try to talk with him as soon as possible to make sure he isn't too depressed or angry over his injury, and that he's going to cooperate with the doctors and physical therapists.

Occasionally, an athlete will get into trouble in his personal life: A paternity suit is filed against him, or he gets into a fistfight or trouble with illegal drugs. Then I have to meet with him and a team lawyer to help him get through it. Even if it's not the kind of problem that legally keeps him from playing, it still might be a distraction, so the team is willing to use its resources to help him.

I often have to be at the games, though not always. I have to stay on top of my schedule, so my wife knows when I have to be at night games or away games (although I go to fewer of those than the home games).

I can usually dress casually at work, which is a plus for me. The athletes seem to prefer talking to me when I don't look like one of the "suits" in the front office, although there are situations when I have to wear a suit—usually if it's an occasion when the lawyer has to be there, too!

Remember that line in *Grease* when the principal tries to boost school spirit and reminds the kids that if they can't be athletes, they can still be athletic supporters? I'm reminded of that line a lot in my line of work. Sports psychology is a great field—no pun intended—for a fan with more brains than brawn who wants to help support the athletes in their quest to reach higher.

STATISTICS ABOUT THIS JOB

The average salary for sports psychologists is approximately $50,000, but can range from $25,000 to $100,000. Sports psychologists who work for a particular team usually get excellent medical benefits designed to protect the athletes' health.

Marianne, Forensic Psychologist

If you've seen the psychologists who work with the lawyers on *Law & Order,* then you probably have some idea of what I do. I'm a forensic psychologist who works for the court system. I started off wanting to become a lawyer like my father and decided to get a psychology degree for my undergraduate degree. When studying psychology, I became more interested in these topics, while at the same time worrying about the stress of the life of a typical trial lawyer. I still liked law, and I wanted to be involved in some way, so I looked into a field that combines both psychology and law and became a forensic psychologist.

What I Do

As a psychologist who works for the court system, I evaluate witnesses and defendants and sometimes testify about their mental capacity or emotional state. I don't administer treatment, but I do make recommendations as to whether someone needs it! For instance, I may interview victims, witnesses, or suspects. I help evaluate witnesses to determine (as much as possible) whether they are lying, whether they can recall the testimony with accuracy, and whether they are capable—meaning whether they are of sound mind—to testify.

Why I Majored in Psychology

I originally wanted to become a lawyer like my father. Because law wasn't a major at my college (most law students come to law school with a variety of undergraduate degrees), I took psychology because I thought it would help me understand the people lawyers have to work with: clients, defendants, witnesses, judge, jury, and, of course, other lawyers!

After a while, I found that I was more interested in practicing psychology than in practicing law, although I was still interested in both. I looked at the lifestyles of some of the trial lawyers I knew, with the long hours and the ulcers and the aggravation, and I knew I didn't want that for myself. But I still liked law, and I wanted to be involved in some way. I had seen psychologists testify in court when I visited my father at work. He asked some of them if they would talk to me.

How My Psychology Major Prepared Me for My Job

I started college thinking that psychology would help me be a good lawyer. Instead, I became a psychologist, so it goes without saying that my major in psychology (with law in mind) was good preparation!

Learning about how to conduct psychological interviews was good preparation for my job. The people I interview are often victims or suspects, and they're not always thrilled about having a court-appointed shrink assessing them. So it takes a lot of finesse to get them to cooperate with me. I also learned about the defensive behaviors people can exhibit when they're traumatized—or when they're lying or not certain they can remember correctly. This information helps me determine whether my witnesses are honest, whether they're of sound enough mind to know what they're talking about, and whether they should even be allowed to testify.

Learning about the ethical practice of psychology was also important. The public knows about doctor-patient confidentiality, but things are much different in forensic psychology. After all, I don't have clients come to me. I have people referred to me by the court or the lawyers, and my job is to report back to them. I'm paid by the department, not by the people I assess. On the other hand, there are other ethical considerations, like how I draw out a witness' responses. My methodology has to be above suspicion, or my report may not be admissible in court. I also have to consider whether my assessment of a witness will affect whether a criminal stands trial and gets convicted.

WHAT OTHER EDUCATION, TRAINING, AND EXPERIENCES I PURSUED

When I began to consider this career switch from lawyer to psychologist, I spoke with some of the forensic psychologists my father introduced me to, and I learned what they had to do to prepare for this career. They also told me about the Forensic Psychology division of the APA (see the appendix for information on this resource) and helped me get a student membership. I was able to get a summer internship with one of the forensic psychologists who knew my father, and it was a great experience. I got a better idea of what professionals in this field do every day, and how it differs from what you see on TV. For example, I don't actually testify in court as often as the psychologists you see on *Law & Order,* although I do sometimes. Usually, my written reports are enough for the court's purposes.

Forensic psychologists do need graduate degrees and other credentials in order to be accepted as experts by the court. With the recommendations of the people I worked with at my internship, I was lucky enough to get into a good program at an institution that specializes in issues of criminal justice. In fact, many of the people from my internship—and not just the psychologists—had gone there, too.

I took classes full-time during my first year and a half of graduate school, and picked up my masters *en passant* (in passing) on the way to the doctorate. After that, I had fewer class hours so that I could start doing the required fieldwork, and my mentors from my college internship were nice enough to welcome me back. Until I finish my degree, I have to work under the supervision of the senior psychologists, but we've known each other a long time, and we have a good relationship. They know what they can expect from me, and I know what they want me to do, so I have a reasonable amount of freedom.

When I'm done with my doctorate, I plan to become board certified through the American Board of Forensic Psychology (see the appendix for information on this resource). This will enable me to join the staff full-time as a full-fledged forensic psychologist. I can't wait!

WHAT HELPED ME SUCCEED

Two things helped me succeed: connections and hard work.

◆ Even though I must sound like Daddy's little princess because my father did help make all of this possible by introducing me to his connections, you can find someone to help mentor you. I realize that not everyone has parents who know people in the field, but I recommend finding someone, even if it's not a family member, who can introduce you to the right people. It really helps make you stand out from all the people your potential mentor meets all day and encourages him or her to take a personal interest in you.

◆ I also recommend learning how to take advantage of an internship. Pay attention! I got a lot information from watching professionals in action. Also, get to know the people with whom you are working. By the time I was ready to apply for a paid position, the people there already knew me. Work hard and do what's asked of you. From my work as an intern, the staff knew that I was motivated and a hard worker, so they were willing to hire me because I had already proven myself.

PITFALLS TO AVOID

Although knowing someone with the right connections who can make the right introductions is great, you have to be prepared to follow up and get there on your own merits. Otherwise, you've not only wasted a great opportunity, but also embarrassed the person who recommended you. That doesn't mean you have to be 100 percent dedicated to a career—or pretend you are—if you're really just trying to learn more about a career. You can be honest and tell people that you're just testing the waters at this point, and that you appreciate the fact that your "hosts" are taking time out from their day to answer your questions. Just respect the time they're giving you. Show up when and where you said you would, dress appropriately, and look alert.

What I Love About My Job

One undeniable thing about me is that I'm naturally curious about people. I love having a job that allows me to satisfy my curiosity about people's motivations and behavior, while at the same time I'm continuing the family tradition of working in the legal field. Some people get into trouble because of their curiosity, but I've found a way to put it to good use, trying to help the wheels of justice run smoothly.

I don't see clients or patients over a long period of time the way therapists do. Sometimes I wish I could follow up with someone, but at least I get more closure with each case. I know that someone is being sent for treatment as I recommended, or that another person will be put on trial, or that I've protected a crime victim from an even worse situation.

Things on the Job I Could Do Without

The paperwork gets to me after a while, and as the youngest psychologist in the office, I get stuck with a lot of it. The administrative assistant has to help the senior guys first and doesn't always have time for me. And some of the bureaucracy is also very frustrating. For instance, determining who pays for a consultation usually is an arguable point. Does the D.A.'s office pay? The plaintiff? The court itself? This issue isn't always clear, particularly because different parties may bring me into the argument in any given case.

In addition to paperwork, I also deal with being pressured to change my opinion. Although I don't have to testify in court often, I do have to speak on the record with lawyers a lot, even if it's just in someone's conference room. It's bad enough when the lawyers who bring me into a case try to push me into bending my professional opinion to help their case, but I am even more annoyed by those who think that because I'm a young woman I can't possibly know what I'm talking about. They try to make me blush or lose my temper, or they flirt with me or talk down to me, almost like baby talk, and I just want to tell them off. Other lawyers ask me ridiculous questions, like when they ask me to apply a statement I've made to some impossible theoretical situation, knowing that there's no way I can answer it. I'm learning which lawyers to watch out for and which ones will stand up for me if the opposing counsel goes too far.

My Work Schedule and Lifestyle

My day includes consultations in my office and in hospitals or prisons, if the person I'm assessing can't come to me for obvious reasons. I meet with the lawyers and other relevant people first to discuss what they need me to find out, and later to review my findings. On rare occasions, I have to testify in court about someone's mental capacity or other psychological matters. The nice thing is that all of this takes place during the normal workday. The trial day ends long before regular business hours do, and even if a crime or an arrest happens in the middle of the night, I don't get called in until the next day. I don't have to go rushing to the scene to talk someone off a ledge or anything like that—at least not so far!

Right now, this works very well for me, because I still have coursework to finish, and my classes at this point tend to be in the late afternoon or early evening, so there's no conflict. Because my professional work and my school work are so closely related, I can discuss class assignments with my co-workers and I can ask my professors technical questions about things that happen at work, as long as I'm discreet.

After I finish my doctorate, I'll be qualified to be called in on the more complex or sensitive cases and to testify as an expert witness on more theoretical matters. That means I may be asked to explain various psychological phenomena that are relevant to a case, not just to present my assessment of an individual.

I like the fact that, despite having such an interesting job, I still have time for a personal life. I've seen how hard my father has worked all these years, and I've heard him take late-night phone calls about his cases, and although I admire his dedication, I'm glad I can regularly have dinner at a normal hour!

Forensic psychology is a good fit for someone who wants to use psychology in the interest of serving justice. It calls for a different outlook than other specialties within psychology, and special skills, such as the ability to make quick yet supportable assessments of people you may only get to interview once.

Statistics About This Job

The average annual salary for forensic psychologists working in the public sector is about $48,600. Those working in private settings may earn considerably more.

Eric, Corporate Psychologist

Have you ever wondered how a specific product was introduced into a market? Well, as a corporate psychologist, I gather information on customers' needs and share it with the designers and engineers so that we can make a product that people will want to buy and use. Initially I was interested in advertising, but because my college did not have an advertising major, I majored in psychology with a minor in business. This lead to my career as a corporate psychologist, which I found out about through a college recruiter.

What I Do

I work in product development for a manufacturing firm. My job is to gather information on customers' needs and share it with the designers and engineers so that we can make a product people will want to buy. This specialty is also called *engineering psychology*, although I'm not an engineer. It's also related to *market research*, but I'm more closely involved in the product-design aspect than most marketing people. I organize focus groups and questionnaires to review new products. I then tabulate and analyze the results, helping the company to decide whether to go forward with a product as planned, alter the product, or kill the product. That's one of the downsides of the job: Sometimes I have to tell them that their brilliant idea is not what consumers want!

Why I Majored in Psychology

In college, I was interested in advertising, so I decided to pursue a psychology major and a business minor. I did it this way (psych major/business minor) because the psychology major also allowed me to take lab courses that fulfilled the university's science requirement, and the labs have prerequisites, so I ended up having to take a lot more credits in psychology than in business. When my roommate heard why I was doing a psychology major, he joked that I just wanted to learn how to manipulate people! Advertising can be manipulative, I guess, but I prefer to think of it as learning how to convince people to buy your product.

How My Psychology Major Prepared Me for My Job

The research skills I learned were the most important thing for this job. I learned how to formulate questions for focus groups and question-naires, how to tabulate and analyze the results, and how to present the results to my colleagues and superiors. I learned to be a better listener and draw out people's responses. I even learned how to tell the engineers about my findings without upsetting them.

What Other Education, Training, and Experiences I Pursued

I didn't go on for any further degrees after college. I figured I didn't need that to go into advertising. Besides, I had to take out loans for college, and I wanted to get them out of the way. But the year I graduated, the job market was pretty bad. All through my senior year, I was sending out resumes and not getting any responses. So I went to a recruitment ses-sion for seniors on campus, hoping I could use all that psychology to convince someone to hire me!

One of the recruiters I met was from a company I eventually went to work for. He told me that they were looking for college graduates with psychology majors to help them understand the public's wishes and improve the company's products. I had never thought about this kind of work before (I'm not sure I even knew about it!), but I was interested right away. He told me that there is a branch of psychology for this kind of thing, and he even showed me some literature from the APA division that represents the field. He made an appointment with me for an interview and some kind of aptitude test right on campus (part of the recruitment-fair procedure). He liked the results, so he asked me to come in to the company's offices for an interview with the higher-ups. I did, and they offered me a job!

I worked there after college for a couple of years, and then I moved on to a couple of other companies, doing the same kind of work. I learned a lot on the job, and I also learned a lot from going to seminars in the field, where I could find out about new developments and resources.

WHAT HELPED ME SUCCEED

Like many students I thought I knew what I wanted to do, but ended up doing something I'd never even heard of. What helped me succeed, I think, are the following ideas (ideas that are relevant to any psychology major in any career):

◆ Even though I wasn't absolutely devoted to advertising, I think it was important that I had a direction when I started college. I knew that I wanted to start earning money right after college, and I had a good idea of the skills I had to offer.

◆ Even though I *thought* I wanted to go into advertising, I was still flexible. I was realistic about the job market, and I was willing to listen to different ideas from recruiters (or whomever). Being rigid and insisting on doing things one way would have meant missing an opportunity and wasting a lot more time trying to find my "dream job."

◆ Using the college's job-hunting resources was also smart. Even when I was applying to all those advertising agencies, I used listings supplied by the career office to find the agencies and learn about them and any job openings. Best of all, I went to the recruitment fair to make personal contact with recruiters and to learn about other job possibilities.

PITFALLS TO AVOID

Like advertising, manufacturing isn't always the most stable business. You have to be prepared for company upheavals. If a product flops, the firm can lose a lot of money and lay people off or close down altogether. One firm can be bought out by a larger company and merge personnel. Even one division within a huge corporation can be sold to a competitor or get disbanded. Be prepared for the possibility of losing your job through no fault of your own. Keep your resume ready, and keep up with people you've worked with in the past. They may end up working on a great new product and want to bring you in on it.

What I Love About My Job

I never considered being an engineer, but as a kid, I always had fun building things with blocks and LEGOs and all of that. Helping to design new products is the same kind of fun, although I leave the really technical stuff to the actual engineers. We play around with prototypes and have a great time—and get paid for it! One special perk is that I get to take home some of that stuff we've been playing with at work. The kid in me really loves collecting all those odds and ends!

I also like meeting consumers and finding out what they want out of a product. I have a lot of great conversations with them. Then I get together with the designers and engineers to tell them what I found.

I really like the place I'm currently working. The people are easy to work with and great to be around, and the office is a really comfortable, non-stuffy place to work.

Things on the Job I Could Do Without

It's nerve-wracking waiting to see whether the new product will succeed or whether the company will collapse under the weight of a failure, leaving us all looking for new jobs. This was how I lost my second job.

In the case of my first job, the company was being bought out, and there was a lot of uncertainty about whether there would be pay cuts, layoffs, or even relocation to another city. As the junior guy in the office, I decided not to wait around, and I started contacting people I knew in the field and sending out resumes again.

The field also may not be lucrative enough for people who want to make a lot of money. Sure, if a product takes off, you may be paid bonuses and raises and things like that. Like advertising, the pay is livable, but not great.

On a more petty level, there are some designers and engineers who get so invested in their own ideas that they reject anyone else's input. I can come in with data showing that buyers want something changed, and these guys will just dismiss my research, sometimes a little too intensely. I guess that's the down side of the "kid" aspect of this business—people can act so childish in the middle of a professional setting!

MY WORK SCHEDULE AND LIFESTYLE

The product development department where I work now is a fairly casual place. Everyone's on a first-name basis, and we wear comfortable clothes, so it's okay to get down on the floor with a design prototype, crawl around it, and get close even when the paint is wet. I keep a slightly more dignified change of clothes on hand for when I do interviews and focus groups.

I don't have to be in too early in the morning, which is fine with me! On the other hand, we usually end up working a little later than people in traditional 9-to-5 settings. When we're really onto a good idea, we don't want to stop! Also, I sometimes have to schedule my data gathering sessions after the people in our target audience are finished with their workday.

I spend part of my day working alone, part of it with my colleagues, and part of it with that target audience. When I'm alone, I'm at my desk creating an interview protocol or questionnaire for the current project, or using the computer to crunch the numbers and put the results together. When I'm with my co-workers, we work on the various steps involved in creating (or improving) a product, from the initial idea to mockups to prototypes and refinements. Along the way, I get my "assignment," so I'll know what kind of questions to ask people when I do my research. When I'm with the target audience, I'm either with a focus group, interviewing people individually, or administering a questionnaire. Depending on the situation, I might ask them to compare two or more products, or I might show them a prototype and ask for their reactions.

This job requires a balance of zaniness and seriousness, of flexibility and discipline. Likewise it requires the ability to work both alone and in a group. If you have this balance, this could be the career for you.

STATISTICS ABOUT THIS JOB

The median salary for a corporate psychologist in the United States is $63,700, with an approximate range of $37,000 to $113,000. A doctorate degree and certification is typically required for this career.

Carlos, Community Psychologist

With the change in demographics in cities and communities, community relations have become an important issue for society. In particular, our community has become increasingly diverse in recent years, and I am part of a team of different specialists who work together to ease the resulting tensions. My reason for pursuing psychology was because of a personal influence; the school psychologist at my school ran a support groups for kids in similar situations (single-parent homes). This person listened to me, and even reached out to help my family. I knew I wanted to study psychology.

I initially intended to follow the path of my mentor and become a school psychologist, but at the time of my graduation, schools were experiencing budget cuts in that area, so I learned about a new opportunity, community psychologist, through a school-sponsored career fair.

What I Do

I work for my local government as part of a team of different specialists who work to ease the resulting tensions of many diverse cultures living together in a community. My role includes helping the mayor and other officials understand the special concerns of the different racial, ethnic, and religious groups; the children and the elderly; the rich and the poor; the disabled and the healthy; and the gays and lesbians in our community. In addition to bringing up special concerns, I advise our leaders on how to reach out to these groups. I also participate in the development of government programs to help make them as appealing as possible for the people who will be served and affected by them.

Why I Majored in Psychology

I grew up in a single-parent household, and one of my lifelines was the school psychologist. Here was a grownup who took the time to listen to me, and even reached out to my family to help all of us work things out together. I thought that was a great thing to do with your life—help people feel better about themselves and each other and help families communicate better to solve their problems. So when I started thinking about a college major, I knew I wanted to study psychology.

When I started taking all those psych courses in college, I also found that some of them helped me understand myself and my family better. For example, when I took developmental psychology, I could see how my developmental tasks were affected by the stuff that was going on in my family at all those stages. I guess you could say I was getting a career education and therapy all at the same time!

How My Psychology Major Prepared Me for My Job

I think I learned a lot of valuable skills as a psychology major. Just the names of the classes I took will give you an idea: developmental psychology, abnormal psychology, conflict resolution and mediation, psychology in minority populations, gerontology, and so on. All of this not only helped me understand what's going on in other people's heads but also how to work with their ways of thinking to bring out the best in their relationships. So now I know how to mediate with people of all ages, with different psychological problems and different cultural identities, just from the courses I took!

What Other Education, Training, and Experiences I Pursued

At first, I assumed I would be a school psychologist, too, like the one from when I was growing up, so I planned on going to graduate school. But as I was exposed to more ideas, both in my classes and from the other students, I started to feel like I wanted to work not just with kids, but with people at all stages of life. My decision was also affected by word that the city schools had budget cuts, and they were cutting back on things like the size of the psychology staff. It didn't seem like an auspicious time to start training to be a school psychologist!

My college hosted a recruiting event for psych majors, so I went. That's when I found out that there even was such a thing as community psychology. Some people came from the mayor's office and told us that, because of the rise in ethnic tensions and bias-related incidents in town, they decided to put together a team of different specialists who could work together on solutions to these problems. They had a basic team of more experienced professionals, but they wanted to bring in some young blood, too, for energy, fresh ideas, and diversity. I thought this was a very exciting concept, and when they told me the city would cover my graduate-school expenses at one of the local institutions so that I could get my master's and work on the team at the same time, I was sold!

The senior psychologist on the team met with me every week while I was in graduate school. We talked about my progress, which classes to sign up for, and even research projects that I could do for school right there at work. Like the school psychologist when I was a kid, here was a professional who helped me make the most of my opportunities and of the resources available to me. That was exactly the kind of thing I wanted to help the team do for the community.

What Helped Me Succeed

People and opportunities helped me. And if you look for them, they'll be available to you, regardless of your career choice. In particular, I think the following helped me to succeed:

◆ I was blessed that two different psychologists took an interest in me and gave me the right kind of guidance. They truly made a difference in my life. Without them, I could've wound up another depressed kid with no goals. So the best advice I can give to students is to find good mentors who really care and with whom you feel comfortable talking.

◆ Another smart move for me was being realistic. I didn't come from a rich family that could send me to some expensive private school. If I wanted to make something of myself, I had to take advantage of the opportunities that came my way. I couldn't say, "Oh, this school is beneath me," or, "I'm too good for this job." When I found out that they weren't going to be hiring new psychologists at the public schools, I was realistic enough to look for other options. So I went to the career center at school and found out about the recruiting fair. I read the materials the recruiters gave me. When I learned about the opportunity to work on the new city program while I worked on my master's degree, and found out they'd pay for it, I was realistic again. I knew it would be hard work and a lot of hours, being a student and a city employee at the same time, but if I weren't willing to tackle it, I would be giving up the chance to further my education and be part of a great new community program.

PITFALLS TO AVOID

Don't get discouraged. No matter what you do in life, there are going to be hard moments, setbacks, and disappointments. And I'll tell you the truth: There were times when I just sat around feeling sorry for myself, from the times when I was a kid and the other kids had two parents come to school events, to when I realized I might not get a job in my dream career after college. As I said, I was blessed because I had people around me who cared to snap me out of it, but I know how easily I could've let those upsets get the better of me. I saw enough guys drop out of school and get into all kinds of trouble because they gave in to the negative feelings when they were faced with problems. If you start to feel that way, find someone to help, even if it's just a friend who can give you some encouragement.

WHAT I LOVE ABOUT MY JOB

I have two things that I love most about my job. One is getting to know so many different kinds of people. I loved this in college, too, coming from a school with such a diverse student body. I've made so many friends, eaten so much ethnic food, listened to all kinds of music, whether it's from a different culture or played by some handicapped kids who made their own instruments—it's all part of what makes America great!

The other thing I love about my job is seeing how I can make a difference, a positive change, in people's lives and communities. When I figure out a way to reach out to a group of immigrants who are distrustful of government-sponsored health programs, or get opposing religious groups to compromise on using city resources, it's just a great feeling. Just like my old school psychologist, I can help people find ways to overcome their problems and live better lives together.

THINGS ON THE JOB I COULD DO WITHOUT

The city has a lot of resources, but it also has a lot of bureaucracy! Sometimes rules and procedures make a program take twice as long to implement or prevent it from getting off the ground in the first place. Other times, people defend their political turf and get in the way of a good program because it's not for their specific constituents, or they want to use the money for something else. I get really impatient with all of that. Sometimes it takes all my psychological training to restrain myself from losing control in those situations!

My Work Schedule and Lifestyle

Some parts of my schedule are pretty well fixed, because there are certain things I have to attend to every day or every week, including regular staff meetings and, of course, my classes. I finished my master's degree last year, and now I'm thinking about whether I want to go on for the doctorate some day. Not yet—it's good to be out of school and working full-time— but maybe some day. In the meantime, I'm auditing some classes. City employees are allowed to do a certain amount of that free of charge.

Other things I have to do for work are not part of the normal work-day. Some of the programs we develop are presented to the public in the evening, when community members are out of work or school. Some programs run on Saturdays and Sundays when parents can bring their kids. I attend breakfasts, dinners, and information fairs. Some of these things take place during the workday, so I can get out of the office and go into the neighborhoods. I like that—not having to sit at a desk all day!

I make a decent living and get good benefits, working for the city in a professional capacity. I don't make as much as people in the private sector, but there are great perks, like being able to audit classes and eat all that free food!

I know this kind of schedule can be hard on your personal life. There are times when I don't like working on the weekend, and I'd rather just hang out with my friends. Some day, when I have kids, I'll want to keep more regular hours. But I'm not worried. If the program I work for continues to be successful, I'll eventually get a young college graduate of my own to mentor!

Statistics About This Job

The mean annual salary for a community psychologist is approximately $35,800.

Karen, School Psychologist

I decided to major in psychology just because I liked it, not for any career-planning reasons. Also, my decision was influenced by my very traditional parents; they considered psychology a respectable field for me. After college, I focused on my family, until a divorce led me back into the working world. Counseling sessions from a local group helped me plan how to figure out how to best put my education to use. I used my psychology major to pursue a career as a school psychologist.

WHAT I DO

I work in an elementary school, where I help in a variety of ways to improve the mental and emotional well being of the students. My responsibilities include administering tests, observing children's behavior, advising parents and teachers, counseling students individually and in groups, and referring those who need it for further help.

WHY I MAJORED IN PSYCHOLOGY

I've always been a fan of psychological thrillers, so it's only natural that I'd be interested in studying psychology. I decided to major in psychology just because I liked it, not for any career-planning reasons. My parents, who were a bit old-fashioned about women's roles at the time, seemed to approve, as long as I focused more on child development rather than mental disorders. They considered psychology a respectable field for a nice girl like me, and thought it might even help me be a good mother some day! As it turned out, I got engaged during my senior year of college and got married shortly after graduation.

HOW MY PSYCHOLOGY MAJOR PREPARED ME FOR MY JOB

In the early days of my marriage, I had a clerical job that had very little to do with my degree. This was at a time when employers were hiring young college graduates with liberal arts degrees just for being well rounded, although I could make the case that my psychology training helped me deal more effectively with customers. My husband was finishing graduate school, and my earnings helped us keep things going. Once he was working full time, we started our family. I left my job when I went on maternity leave, and his career took off. While the kids were little, I was able to stay home with them, and when they started elementary school, I volunteered at their school as a class mother and got involved with the PTA.

Then my husband and I got divorced.

We were able to keep things reasonably amicable, but I knew I would have to go back to work full-time. I wanted a job that would be an interesting career for me, while at the same time providing salary, benefits, and hours that would let me do right by my kids. When I assessed my marketable skills, I saw that it would be best to capitalize on my psychology degree, now enhanced by my parenting experience, especially helping my children through the painful process of a divorce.

To me, it made sense to work with children in a psychological capacity. Needless to say, my major gave me a lot of the basic knowledge I would need for my job. I also emphasized my related skills from parenting, including dealing with homework and other academic issues as well as coping with major life events.

What Other Education, Training, and Experiences I Pursued

To be certified as a school psychologist in my state, I had to get my doctorate. I was fortunate enough to find a program at a local university that is designed for older and returning students who need flexible programs. First of all, this type of program will often give credit or waive requirements based on work experience, so I was able to get through graduate school faster, and with fewer courses to work on and pay for. Second, the scheduling was helpful. I was able to work my classes around my children's schedules and take the bulk of my courses when they were at summer camp or visiting their father.

I also had to do a certain number of supervised work hours, both for my degree and my license. Luckily, the flexible program came to the rescue again, and some of my volunteer experience was counted. My volunteer activities involved some of the same skills I was learning about in graduate school, and my children's school principal was willing to be counted as my supervisor. I still had to do additional supervised hours, but not as many.

WHAT HELPED ME SUCCEED

I found a couple of things were key to my success:

♦ When I got divorced, one of the first things I did was attend a counseling program for newly divorced women and women reentering the workforce, held at the community center my family belongs to. The counselor I worked with helped me identify my marketable skills and figure out what to do with them. When I decided to go back to school for a graduate degree, she helped me work out all those little details, like how to pay for it! She was able to direct me to resources, such as the program at the local university, that I was unaware of. I really would have been floundering around helplessly without her guidance.

♦ My experiences at the community center gave me a lot of ideas that I now use at work. I learned a lot from the patient and encouraging demeanor of my career counselor there, and I saw how helpful support groups could be when I joined some at the center. It taught me so much about how to behave with the children at my school, how to do established programs like the "Banana Splits" support group for kids from broken homes, and how to make a comforting and welcoming environment.

PITFALLS TO AVOID

It's very easy to let your schedule get away from you in a situation like mine. Between work and classes and taking care of the kids and the house, something usually gets neglected—often your own personal needs. My career counselor and support group at the community center were so helpful in this area, helping me plan realistically and sharing useful suggestions. I also have to give credit to my kids, who were remarkably patient and cooperative while I was finishing my degree, and even my ex-husband, who accommodated my scheduling issues and contributed to my tuition money without complaint. Admittedly, there were times when I didn't get a haircut for months on end, but I was lucky to have such a supportive network of family and friends.

WHAT I LOVE ABOUT MY JOB

I love working with children, and I get a lot of satisfaction from helping them be happier in their lives. Whether it's a typical childhood squabble, a family problem, or a learning disability, it's all very real to the kids, and they need a caring adult who takes them seriously to help them cope. I'll also admit that I'm very flattered when parents come to me for advice about their children, or when teachers bring their concerns to me, or even when children come running to my office when they're upset. I like knowing that they trust me and my knowledge, and they consider my little corner of the school to be a safe haven.

THINGS ON THE JOB I COULD DO WITHOUT

Oh, I could do without bureaucracy, prejudiced attitudes, and budget constraints—shall I go on?

The bureaucracy is infuriating sometimes because it can insist that I do things that I know are against a child's best interests, or keep me from doing what I know the child needs. For example, I may refer a child for a special program, and the bureaucracy will deny my referral because the child was born two days outside the age range. Other times, I may be asked to report on private sessions that I feel should remain confidential.

Bad attitudes can come from teachers, parents, and even other students. Sometimes teachers expect instant cures for a child they find troublesome, but cures take time, and sometimes there really isn't anything wrong with the kid to begin with! Teachers may also resent it when I pull a student out of class to deal with a non-academic problem.

With parents, the attitude can come from any number of things. Some parents think there's a stigma attached to seeing a school psychologist, so they don't want their child working with me even when there's clearly a need for it. It's hard to get through to them that seeing the school psychologist doesn't mean that the child is mentally ill or even that there's anything wrong at all! And if there *is* something wrong, it would be terrible to ignore it out of fear of "what people will think!" And, of course, the most aggravating thing of all is when it's the parents themselves who are causing their children's problems.

Students, of course, can make the problem worse by teasing, bullying, and spreading rumors. One way I've tried to counter this is by making myself known to as many of the kids as possible and being available as a mentor and sounding board, so the children will know that I'm not just there to handle the "crazies." I talk to them about the events in their lives, even if it's nothing traumatic, to show not only that I care, but that not everyone they see walking into my office is there for some bad reason—we might just be chatting about their new baby at home!

Money for programs or testing can also be a problem. When I feel that a student needs further testing or special help, these requests cost money, and there may not be enough to pay a specialist or buy materials. While the law may guarantee a free and appropriate education to every child, the budget unfortunately doesn't always follow through.

My Work Schedule and Lifestyle

As a single mom, I really appreciate the fact that I'm more or less on the same school day schedule as my own kids. They're in upper school now, in a different building, but I can pick them up on the way home, or at least be home when they are, and I'm free to spend time with them in the evenings.

My financial situation is better than I thought it would be. My doctorate entitles me to a higher salary scale, and as a faculty member, I get good healthcare benefits for me and my children.

Working in a school setting like this made it possible for me to get established in my new career a lot faster than I could have in private practice. I didn't have to build up a client base or even rent office space; the school provided the clients, the office, and even the salary right from the start!

I think this career is suited for psychology majors who enjoy working with children, are patient and compassionate, can deal with bureaucracy and a range of individuals (teachers, students, principals, parents), and most of all want to make a difference in a child's life.

Statistics About This Job

The median salary for school psychologists in the United States is $51,170, with an approximate range of $39,000 to $70,000. Most school systems require a graduate degree and several years of experience in the field.

Resources

This appendix includes several other resources that are helpful for finding out more about psychology majors and careers. You'll find Web sites, books, career counseling and personality testing information, professional societies, and more.

American Psychological Association

Contact Information
750 First Street, NE
Washington, DC 20002-4242
Phone: 800-374-2721 or 202-336-5500
TDD/TTY: 202-336-6123
Web site: www.apa.org

The most important organization for psychology majors is the American Psychology Association (APA). This organization includes more than 150,000 members and is the largest association of psychologists in the world. Joining the APA is a great way to network with other members, to find out about new developments in your field, to seek out internship or employment opportunities, to attend conferences or other training in your field, and much more. The APA publishes numerous books, newsletters, and journals. (See the section on "Journals and Books" later in this appendix for a list of some of their publications.)

You can choose from a variety of membership options, depending where you are in your schooling and career. For instance, you can find memberships for everyone from high school students to teachers, from undergraduates to graduates, from professional psychologists and "fellows," chosen for membership based on their outstanding achievements.

Members also have access to special online databases and online tools (such as a member directory); they also receive a variety of print, audio, video, and multimedia publications. The public has access to some, but not all, of the tools available to members.

The APA Web site contains the organization's mission statement, a five-pronged approach to encouraging and endorsing the further study of psychology and psychological research in all areas.

The APA currently recognizes 53 professional divisions; these give you some idea of the different fields or areas you may study or specialize in. Check out the Division home page for a list of the 53 professional divisions (http://www.apa.org/about/division.html).

Honor Societies

Psi Chi, the National Honor Society in Psychology
National Office:
P.O. Box 709
Chattanooga, TN 37401-0709
Phone: 423-756-2044
Web site: www.psichi.org

The National Honor Society in Psychology, or Psi Chi, is one of the most active psychology organizations on campuses. If you are a psychology major, you are highly encouraged to join and participate. While one of its goals is to recognize students who are doing well academically, the society also seeks to help develop opportunities for its members to network and gain experience. The society sponsors programs, hosts research competitions, and holds national conferences. It also publishes a quarterly magazine, *Eye on Psi Chi,* to keep its members informed and to recognize achievement of its members. Finally, Psi Chi provides over $225,000 annually in awards and grants to its student members, faculty advisers, and chapters.

Membership is open to undergraduates and graduates and the criteria vary depending on whether you are an undergraduate or a graduate. If you're an undergraduate, you must have completed a set number of semesters or quarters, rank in the top 35 percent of your class in general scholarship, and have a minimum GPA of 3.0—on a 4.0 scale—in both psychology and other grades. You can check the requirements as well as membership costs (currently $35 for a lifetime membership) by visiting the Psi Chi Web site (www.psichi.org).

Psi Beta, National Honor Society in Psychology for Community and Junior Colleges
National Office:
1027 Westbridge Lane
Chattanooga, TN 37405-4274
Phone: 888-PSI-BETA (774-2382) or 423-645-8205
Fax: 423-265-0033
Web site: www.psibeta.org

The mission of Psi Beta is "professional development of psychology students in two-year colleges through promotion and recognition of excellence in scholarship, leadership, research, and community service." Because students at two-year colleges are not eligible for membership in Psi Chi, Psi Beta was formed in 1981 and has expanded to 175+ chapters and over 20,000 members. It publishes the *Psi Beta Newsletter* three times a year. Membership requirements and member benefits are similar to Psi Chi, with adjustments made for the two-year college experience.

The American Board of Professional Psychology (Certification)

Contact Information:
300 Drayton Street, 3rd Floor
Savannah, GA 31401
Phone: 800-255-7792
Fax: 912-644-5655
Web site: www.abpp.org

The American Board of Professional Psychology's (ABPP) main purpose is to certify psychologists in various specialty areas of psychology. When someone is board certified, that person, according to the ABPP, "has successfully completed the educational, training, and experience requirements of the specialty, including an examination designed to assess the competencies required to provide quality services in that specialty."

The ABPP includes 13 boards, each one representing a specialty.

Other Professional Organizations and Resources

The following sections discuss some additional organizations, including those relating to the case studies in Chapter 7. Keep in mind that this resource appendix, while covering the most important and common resources, only provides a glimpse at the many different organizations, associations, and resources you can find within the field of psychology. Look for other organizations during your studies or readings. Also, if you are looking for a particular organization or club, search for it using one of the Internet's many search tools.

ART THERAPY

American Art Therapy Association (AATA)
1202 Allanson Road
Mundelein, IL 60060-3808
Phone: 888-290-0878 or 847-949-6064
Fax: 847-566-4580
Web site: www.arttherapy.org

The American Art Therapy Association, Inc. (AATA) is the professional organization in the art therapy field. It sets the educational, professional, and ethical standards for practitioners of art therapy. You can find memberships for all stages of a career, from students to retirees. AATA also publishes a research journal, a newsletter, a membership directory, and other print resources, and convenes national and regional conferences to further continuing education in the field.

Art Therapy Credentials Board (ATCB)
3 Terrace Way, Suite B
Greensboro, NC 27403
Phone: 877-213-ATCB (2822)
Fax: 336-482-2852
Web site: http://www.atcb.org

The Art Therapy Credentials Board (ATCB) oversees the registration and board certification of art therapists. The *registered* designation is for those who have successfully completed training at an accredited school, including academic coursework and fieldwork experience. The *board certified* designation is for registered art therapists who have taken and passed the ATCB national certification exam. Art therapists must be recertified every five years through such activities as continuing education courses and publishing and presenting research. The ATCB works in cooperation with the AATA.

To find out more information about art therapy, check out http://www.apa.org/about/division/div10.html.

Sport Psychology

Association for the Advancement of Applied Sport Psychology (AAASP)
AAASP Home Office:
7600 Terrace Avenue, Suite 203
Middleton, WI 53562
Phone: 608-831-0144
Fax: 608-831-5122
Web site: www.aaasponline.org

The Association for the Advancement of Applied Sport Psychology (AAASP) offers certification to qualified practitioners. It publishes a research journal, a newsletter, and professional directories; holds an annual conference; and provides networking and resources for students as well as coaches, athletes, and therapists. You can download applications for certification from the Web site. The Web site also provides email links to the organization's various departments.

American Psychological Association
Exercise and Sport Psychology
750 First Street, NE
Washington, DC 20002-4242
Phone: 800-374-2721 or 202-336-5500
Web site: www.apa.org/about/division/div47.html

The APA's Division 47 is the division for Exercise and Sport Psychology. For students, Division 47 has resources for training opportunities, Listservs, and scholarship and award information. To join Division 47, you need to join the APA. You can find membership information as well as publications and opportunities in this division at the APA Web site at www.apa.org.

FORENSIC PSYCHOLOGY

American Psychological Association
American Psychology-Law Society
750 First Street, NE
Washington, DC 20002-4242
Phone: 800-374-2721 or 202-336-5500
Web site: www.apa.org/about/division/div41.html

The APA's Division 41 is the American Psychology-Law Society. Those who practice psychology in this area are often asked to evaluate witnesses, victims, accused, and other law personnel; they work with the legal system to provide a better psychological understanding of the crime, the people involved, or the environment. This division applies psychology to better understand the law and legal institutions. Members receive the bimonthly journal *Law and Human Behavior* and the *American Psychology-Law Society Newsletter* three times per year.

The American Board of Forensic Psychology (ABFP)
Web site: www.abfp.com

The American Board of Forensic Psychology (ABFP) is the certifying authority for professionals in the field. Qualified applicants can receive a Board diploma if they meet the requirements, which include credentials, a review of their work, and an oral examination by a panel of three psychologists who already hold the diploma. Applicants who succeed in earning the diploma become diplomats and are listed in the ABFP Directory.

The ABFP also runs the American Academy of Forensic Psychology, which offers continuing education workshops around the country to help professionals keep their knowledge up to date and to fulfill their continuing education requirements. You can access both the certification site and the academy site at www.abfp.com.

CORPORATE PSYCHOLOGY

American Psychological Association
Society for Consumer Psychology
750 First Street, NE
Washington, DC 20002-4242
Phone: 800-374-2721 or 202-336-5500
Web site: www.apa.org/about/division/div23.html

Division 23 of the APA is the Society for Consumer Psychology. This division includes psychologists and other consumer researchers who study profit and non-profit marketing, advertising, communication, and consumer behavior. This division seeks to research scientifically and develop theories that explain how individual and social psychology work together in the consumer exchange of goods or services. This division publishes the *Journal of Consumer Psychology* as well as the *Journal of Consumer Research and Psychology and Marketing*. This division may provide insight into consumer psychology, but you may also try Division 14, Society for Industrial and Organizational Psychology, for additional information.

COMMUNITY PSYCHOLOGY

American Psychological Association
Society for Community Research and Action:
Division of Community Psychology
750 First Street, NE
Washington, DC 20002-4242
Phone: 800-374-2721 or 202-336-5500
Web site: www.apa.org/about/division/div27.html

Division 27 of the APA is the Society for Community Research and Action: Division of Community Psychology. The psychologists in this division look at how individuals work within the social system or community. Their goals include promoting of "social and behavioral science to enhance the well-being of people and their communities and to prevent harmful outcomes," striving to liberate oppressed people, teaching respect for all individuals and cultures, and promoting careers and educational opportunities in the community. Members receive two publications: *American Journal of Community Psychology* (published bimonthly) and *The Community Psychologist* (published five times per year).

SCHOOL PSYCHOLOGY

American Psychological Association
Division of School Psychology
750 First Street, NE
Washington, DC 20002-4242

Phone: 800-374-2721 or 202-336-5500
Web site: www.apa.org/about/division/div16.html

The Division of School Psychology brings together professionals who work with children, families, and the schooling process so that they can improve their skills as individuals. These psychologists also seek to look at the educational field as it relates to child psychology and to lobby for reform in education and health care when needed. Like other divisions, members of the Division of School Psychology receive the journal, *School Psychology Quarterly,* and a newsletter called *The School Psychologist.*

Other Psychology Associations and Organizations

American Counseling Association
5999 Stevenson Avenue
Alexandria, VA 22304
Phone: 800-347-6647
Fax: 800-473-2329
Web site: www.counseling.org

The American Counseling Association is a non-profit association "dedicated to the growth and enhancement of the counseling profession." The group provides leadership training and continuing education opportunities. It is also key in setting the professional and ethical standards for the counseling profession and appears before Congress and federal agencies to support and represent the interest of the profession.

Association for Behavioral Analysis
1219 South Park Street
Kalamazoo, MI 49001
Phone: 269-492-9610
Fax: 269-492-9616
Web site: www.abainternational.org

The mission statement of the Association for Behavioral Analysis (ABA) is to "develop, enhance, and support the growth and vitality of behavior analysis through research, education, and practice." Different levels of membership are offered, including a student membership, with benefits including periodicals, reduced convention fees, and access to the job placement service.

Association for Women in Psychology
Web site: www.awpsych.org

The Association for Women in Psychology (AWP) was founded in 1969 as a "not-for-profit scientific and educational organization committed to encouraging feminist psychological research, theory, and activism." It is organized into regional, state, and local chapters. Reduced membership fees are available for students and others of limited means. Membership benefits include grants and awards; publications including a newsletter, directory, and Listservs; and opportunities to serve as a liaison or participate in caucuses such as Caucus on Bisexuality and Sexual Diversity, Jewish Women's Caucus, and Women of Color Caucus. This association also gives you access to a network of 2,000+ feminist scientists, educators, mental health professionals, and activists.

American Association for Marriage and Family Therapy
112 South Alfred Street
Alexandria, VA 22314
Phone: 703-838-9808
Fax: 703-838-9805
Web site: www.aamft.org

As the professional association for the field of marriage and family therapy, American Association for Marriage and Family Therapy represents the interests of its members: currently more than 23,000 marriage and family therapists throughout the United States, Canada, and abroad. The association seeks both to increase the understanding, research, and education in this field of therapy, as well as to promote its members, providing them with tools and resources to improve their practice or education. Finally, this association develops "standards for graduate education and training, clinical supervision, professional ethics and the clinical practice of marriage and family therapy."

American Mental Health Counselors Association
801 N. Fairfax Street, Suite 304
Alexandria, VA 22314
Phone: 800-326-2642 or 703-548-6002
Fax: 703-548-4775
Web site: www.amhca.org

The mission of the American Mental Health Counselors Association is "to enhance the profession of mental health counseling through licensing, advocacy, education and professional development." The organization helps its members with all aspects of this mission: to locate and get licensed by their state board and to provide ample opportunities for leadership, advocacy, and additional education and training opportunities.

Journals and Books

Many organizations and associations publish journals. (Some of the many APA journals are listed below.) In addition, you can find other publications helpful for your career and college studies. You can also find a wealth of books on the topic of psychology (every division, aspect, and topic!), on psychology majors, on picking a college, on getting into graduate school, on finding a job (creating the perfect resume, handling the interview, finding jobs online, and more). This section lists just a few key books.

Remember to check your psychology department as well as your career center; they often have subscriptions to these journals. Career and job advice books are often housed in the career center library. Don't neglect the university library either; it's likely to have a wealth of resources.

JOURNALS

The APA's purpose is to advance psychology as a science and profession, and it provides a vast amount of information in the various journals it publishes within its 53 divisions. You can find information about these publications on the organization's Web site. If you are a member of the APA, you may receive these journals. You can also try to buy more popular ones at newsstands or through the APA.

BOOKS FOR FURTHER READING

Careers in Psychology: Opportunities in a Changing World by Tara L. Kuther and Robert D. Morgan; Wadsworth Publishing; August 2003 ISBN: 053461776X. A companion to *The Psychology Major's Handbook,* aimed at those considering graduate school.

Career Paths in Psychology: Where Your Degree Can Take You by Robert J. Sternberg (Editor); American Psychological Association (APA); 1st edition, January 15, 1997; ISBN: 1557984115. Fourteen articles on different psychology professions, written by practitioners in each field.

Graduate Programs in Psychology 2004 (Peterson's Decision Guides: Graduate Programs) by Peterson's Guides; 4th edition, May 2003; ISBN: 076891194X. A collaborative effort of Peterson's and the Educational Testing Service (ETS), which puts out the Graduate Record Exam (GRE) for grad school admissions. This guide is updated every year.

Graduate Study in Psychology 2004 (Graduate Study in Psychology) by American Psychological Association (Editor); July 1, 2003; ISBN: 1591470579. An annual guide published by the APA, this directory-style book describes psychology graduate departments and schools in both the U.S. and Canada.

The Psychology Major's Handbook by Tara L. Kuther. Wadsworth Publishing; 1st edition, July 23, 2002; ISBN: 0155085115. A guide to preparing for a major and career in psychology, including study and other academic advice, as well as an overview of the professions within the field. Also offers a self-assessment test.

Self-Administered Aptitude Tests

With the wealth of information on the Internet, you can find not only all kinds of career advice, but also assessment tests that evaluate your type of personality, your particular skills and talents, and other qualities. Keep in mind that these tests are based on your answers to the questions. If you answer, how you think *you should* answer, the results aren't going to be valid. Answer honestly. Also, these tests give general advice and descriptions; there is no way to determine what type of person you are based on an online assessment. Still, they can give you some insight into your interests and abilities.

Keep in mind that some tests are provided for free. Some provide a mini-review based on your responses, and you can then pay for a more detailed analysis. And some charge a fee to even take the test. Whether it costs money and how much money are not necessarily the best ways to evaluate the effectiveness of the test. Instead, read about the test.

What research is it based on? Who developed the test? What is the scientific theory behind the testing? Reading this information will allow you to better assess the test.

Also, taking the test can be fun (and addicting!). Everyone likes to know more about himself or herself. Explore the available testing and use it as *one* aspect in making your decision. (Aptitude tests can help not only with choosing a major, but also with finding a career suitable to your personality.)

The most popular career tests include:

◆ Strong Interest Inventory (SII)

◆ Myers-Briggs Type Indicator (MBTI)

◆ Birkman Method

◆ The Enneagram

◆ Kiersey Temperament Sorter

◆ Campbell Interest and Skill Survey (CISS)

◆ System for Interactive Guidance and Information (SIGI)

◆ The Kolbe Assessment

The following sections describe some popular tests and testing sites.

THE PRINCETON REVIEW CAREER QUIZ

Offered by The Princeton Review, you can visit this Web site (www.princetonreview.com) and take its career tests.

JOHN HOLLAND'S SDS (SELF-DIRECTED SEARCH) — RIASEC

Available at www.self-directed-search.com, this test is taken online and costs under $10. Devised by Dr. John Holland, it classifies your answers among six personality traits (Realistic, Investigative, Artistic, Social, Enterprising, and Conventional) and assigns you a three-letter "Holland code," representing the three traits, in order of relevance, that best describe you. An Interpretive Report then lists careers that might interest you, each with further information on such things as the amount of training needed. Similar lists of studies and leisure activities are also in the report. The report even offers lists for other combinations of the three letters in your code, just in case you're curious. The report ends with a list of resources for further information.

CAREER INTERESTS GAME

The Career Interests Game was designed by Dr. Holland's friend Richard Bolles (author of *What Color Is Your Parachute?*) as a brief alternative to the RIASEC SDS. It appears in newer editions of Bolles' books and is also on the University of Missouri Web site at http:// career.missouri.edu, where there is a link to the "game." It's free of charge, so it may be a good way to sample Holland's method before deciding whether to pay for the original, in-depth test and report.

MOTIVATIONAL APPRAISAL OF PERSONAL POTENTIAL (MAPP)

This test asks multiple-choice questions with three possible answers that you rank in order of your preferences. The results of the tests are emailed to you. This test has been widely used not only by individuals, but also by employers, who may use it to determine an applicant's suitability for a job, and by schools and teachers, who may use it to provide better guidance for students. The test can be found at assessment.com. Be warned that the pricing is not readily apparent until you have already "signed on" with your personal information.

MYERS-BRIGGS INVENTORY

A test of personality type, results of the Myers-Briggs Inventory can be applied to relationships and personal growth as well as your career. It is available through several Web sites. Some sites offer the test for free; some provide a quick summary but charge you for a full, in-depth assessment. Some charge a fee just to take the test. At the time of this writing, you could get some free assessments at www.humanmetrics.com, as well as haleonline.com Because these sites change often, the pricing changes, and the sites come and go, you might do best by searching to find sites that offer tests (free or otherwise). Searching can also help you locate a test of particular interest.

KEIRSEY CHARACTER SORTER

This test takes your answers and determines which of the four temperaments (rationalists, artisans, guardians, and idealists) best match your personality (the idea is similar to Enneagram). You can take a sample test and get more information (including ordering books devoted to this test and its personality theory) by visiting www.keirsey.com.

TICKLE.COM

You can find a wealth of useful as well as frivolous tests at Tickle.com. You can, for instance, determine which *Friends* character is most like you. Likewise, you can also determine what rock star you are. In addition to fun tests, the site offers a wealth of useful personality and career testing including:

- ◆ Career Interest Inventory
- ◆ Career Personality Test
- ◆ Right Job, Wrong Job
- ◆ Corporate Culture Test
- ◆ The Confidence Test
- ◆ Social Networking Test

In most cases, the tests are free and come with a basic report of your results. You can get a more in-depth, personalized report for roughly $20. You can also subscribe to the service and take as many tests as you want, getting detailed results for all the tests you take. Experiment, but keep in mind that you don't need a detailed report for every category and test. (Once you get started, it's hard to stop because you want to know more!)

Career Counseling

Although colleges and universities have their own career counseling services, you may prefer an independent service, especially if you are not currently spending time on campus. These services may also reach further in scope, in terms of both target audience (throughout the life span, including pre-college) and study/career fields (for example, they may include subjects not offered at a small or specialized school), although plenty of on-campus services do offer these things. Just remember that because these are commercial services, they will cost you something.

AfterImage Associates, LLC
310 Roosevelt Avenue
Hasbrouck Heights, NJ 07604
Phone: 201-288-0964
Fax: 201-288-0965
Web site: www.afterimagenet.com

AfterImage services include assessment testing (including some of the tests listed above), test prep, and counseling to help you find the school, major, or career path that is best for you. It has an extensive range of price plans and links to many other resources.

The Oxford Program of Career Change
212 County Highway 52
Cooperstown, NY 13326-4921
Phone: 800-959-9183
Web site: www.theoxfordprogram.com

Oxford offers two package deals of testing, personalized online counseling, and placement assistance. The basic program costs $149; the expanded one, for $457, includes an additional Entrepreneur Profile Report and a longer period of ongoing support. Free resources on the site include access to informative articles and links to online and home study courses.

These are just two examples in the New York/New Jersey area. If you want to find someone in your area, ask around for recommendations. Career counseling has seen a burst in popularity and it includes clients of all ages (not just those who have recently graduated). If you can't find someone from a recommendation, look through your local newspaper. You might also look through the Yellow Pages or search on the Internet. If you find some counselors through your own research, call and talk with that person. What services do they provide? What are the fees? What is the background of the counselor? Do they specialize in any particular areas? Also, ask for references (and call and check them).

Index

A

AAASP (Association for the Advancement of Applied Sport Psychology), 109

AAMFT (American Association for Marriage and Family Therapy), 60, 113

AATA (American Art Therapy Association), 108

ABA (Association for Behavioral Analysis), 112–113

ABFP (American Board of Forensic Psychology), 110

abilities/skills
  major selection, 10
  psychology major requirements, 15–18

ABPP (American Board of Professional Psychology), 107

academic challenges, major selection, 10

activities
  college selection element, 26
  networking opportunity, 32–33

adaptability, desirable employee characteristic, 46

addictions counselor, 59, 60

adjunct faculty, college selection element, 25

adult students
  graduate school guidelines, 44
  returning to college, 28

advertising (media buyer), career, 64

advertising (media planner), career, 65

advisors
  college selection element, 26
  graduate school selection element, 41

AIDS counselor, 59, 60

AIDS/HIV Disease and Medicaid, 59

alumni
  college selection element, 26
  job market resource, 50
  networking opportunity, 36

alumni associations, internship resource, 35

AMCHA (American Mental Health Counselors Association), 113–114

American Art Therapy Association (AATA), 108

American Association for Marriage and Family Therapy (AAMFT), 60, 113

American Board of Forensic Psychology (ABFP), 110

American Board of Professional Psychology (ABPP), 107

American Counseling Association, 112

American Mental Health Counselors Association (AMHCA), 60, 113–114

American Psychological Association (APA), 105–106, 110–112

American Psychological Association Division of School Psychology, 111–112

American Psychological Association Exercise and Sport Psychology, 109

American Psychological Association
    Society for Community Research...,
    111
American Psychological Association
    Society for Consumer Psychology,
    110–111
American Psychology-Law Society,
    110–111
AMHCA (American Mental Health
    Counselors Association), 60
analytical skills, desirable employee
    characteristic, 46
anthropology course, psychology major
    integration, 15
APA (American Psychological
    Association), 105–106, 110–112
APA (gradPSYCH), 41
Applications
    colleges/universities, 27
    graduate school, 42–44
Art therapist, case study, 71–78
Art Therapy Credentials Board (ATCB),
    108–109
Association for Behavioral Analysis
    (ABA), 112–113
Association for Women in Psychology
    (AWP), 113
Association for the Advancement of
    Applied Sport Psychology (AAASP),
    109
ATCB (Art Therapy Credentials Board),
    108–109
athletes, college selection resources, 22
AWP (Association for Women in
    Psychology), 113

B

best 110 Internships, 35
biology course, psychology major
    integration, 15
brochures, college selection resource, 20,
    22–23
Bureau of Labor Statistics, 11, 20, 70
business course, psychology major
    integration, 15

C

career advisors
    college selection element, 26
    graduate school selection element,
        41
career centers
    internship resource, 34, 35
    job market resource, 50, 51–52
career counselor, 59, 60
career fairs, job market resource, 51–52
Careerbuilder.com, job-related Web
    site, 49
careers
    addictions counselor, 59, 60
    advertising (media buyer), 64
    advertising (media planner), 65
    AIDS counselor, 59, 60
    art therapist, 71–78
    career counselor, 59, 60
    child psychologist, 61, 63
    child welfare caseworker, 65
    clinical counselor, 59, 60
    clinical psychologist, 61–62, 63
    college professor, 62, 63
    community psychologist, 95–99
    corporate psychologist, 90–94
    counseling psychologist, 62, 63
    counselors, 58–61
    developmental psychologist, 62, 63
    employment counselor (college),
        65–66
    experimental psychologist, 62–63
    family counselor, 60
    forensic psychologist, 84–90
    graduate degree requirements,
        39–40
    hotel manager, 66
    human resources specialist, 66
    industrial psychologist, 63
    insurance agent, 66
    major selection, 11
    market research analyst, 66–67
    marriage counselor, 60
    mental health counselor, 60
    neuropsychologist, 63, 64

organizational psychologist, 63
police officer, 67
psychologists, 62–69
psychology paraprofessional, 67
psychotherapist, 63, 64
public relations specialist, 67
rehabilitation counselor, 60
retail buyer, 68
retail store manager, 68
school psychologist, 100–104
social psychologist, 63, 64
sports psychologist, 78–84
teacher, 68–69
chamber of commerce, job market
    resource, 49
character/personality testing, major
    selection resource, 12
chemistry course, psychology major
    integration, 15
child psychologist, career, 61, 63
child welfare caseworker, career, 65
class planning
    double major considerations, 31
    guidelines, 30–31
    resume considerations, 32
    senior thesis preparation, 31–32
clients, job market resource, 50
clinical counselor, career, 59, 60
clinical psychologist
    career, 61–62, 63
    graduate degree requirement, 39
clothing (dress), interview guidelines, 55
clubs
    college selection element, 26
    networking opportunity, 32–33
college employment counselor, career,
    65–66
college professor, career, 62, 63
colleges
    advice handling techniques, 21–22
    application process, 27
    brochures, 22–23
    consideration list preparation, 22
    major selection resource, 12

psychology major selection criteria,
    25–27
returning after leaving, 28
selection guidelines, 21–25
selection questions, 23–24
transfers, 28
Collegegrad.com, job-related Web site,
    49
committees, networking opportunity,
    32–33
communication skills, desirable
    employee characteristic, 46
community psychologist, case study,
    95–99
companies, job market resource, 52–53
company Web sites, internship resource,
    35
competitors, job market resource, 50
computer skills, desirable employee
    characteristic, 46
conferences, networking opportunity,
    32–33
corporate psychologist, case study,
    90–94
counseling psychologist
    career, 62, 63
    graduate degree requirement, 39
counselors
    college selection resource, 22
    major selection resource, 11
co-workers, job market resource, 50
cultural studies course, psychology
    major integration, 15
customers, job market resource, 50

D

developmental psychologist, career,
    62, 63
discussion courses, psychology major
    element, 14
double majors, class planning
    element, 31
dress (clothing), interview guidelines, 55

E

education course, psychology major
integration, 15
educational psychologist, graduate
degree requirement, 39
employees
desirable characteristics, 46
major selection resource, 12
employers
desirable employee
characteristics, 46
job market resource, 50
employment, job outlook, 20
employment counselor (college), career,
65–66
environmental course, psychology major
integration, 15
experimental psychologist, career, 62–63

F

faculty
college selection element, 25
graduate school selection
element, 40
job market resource, 50
family counselor, career, 60
family/friends
college selection resource, 21–22
job market resource, 50
fields of study
major selection guidelines, 10–11
myths of choosing a major, 8–10
reasons for switching majors, 10
finances, major selection, 11
flexibility, desirable employee
characteristic, 46
Florida State University, March Major
Sheets, 70
follow up interviews, guidelines, 55–56
forensic psychologist, case study, 84–90
friendliness, interview guidelines, 55
friends/family, college selection
resource, 22

G

George Mason University, skill set
suggestions, 18
GradPSYCH (APA), 41
Gradschool.com, graduate school
resource, 41
Graduate Entrance Exam (GRE),
graduate school requirement, 40,
42–43
graduate school
application process, 42–44
college selection considerations,
40–41
cost considerations, 43–44
GRE (Graduate Entrance Exam),
40, 42–43
letters of recommendation, 43
returning students, 44
Graduateguide.com, graduate school
resource, 41
GRE (Graduate Entrance Exam),
graduate school requirement, 40,
42–43

H

handshakes, interview guidelines, 55
history courses, psychology major
integration, 15
honesty, employee characteristic, 46
Hoovers.com, company overviews,
53–54
hotel manager, career, 66
human resources specialist, career, 66

I

industrial psychologist, career, 63
information interviews, networking
opportunity, 37–38
initiative, employee characteristic, 46
insurance agent, career, 66
integrity, employee characteristic, 46
interests, major selection, 10

internet
  college selection resource, 22–23
  internship resource, 35
  job market resources, 49–50
  major selection resource, 12
The Internship Bible, 35
internships
  experience/information
    opportunity, 33–35
  graduate school selection
    element, 41
  major selection resource, 12
interviews
  dress (clothing) guidelines, 55
  follow up, 55–56
  friendly but professional
    attitude, 55
  handshakes, 55
  information, 37–38
  practicing, 54
  preparations, 53–54
  questions (yours), 55–56
  timeliness, 55
introductory course, psychology major
  requirement, 13
IUPUI, psychology survey questions, 13

J

job market
  desirable employee
    characteristics, 46
  information resources, 48–53
  interview guidelines, 53–56
  pre-planning elements, 45–46
  resume preparation guidelines,
    47–48

L

laboratory courses, psychology major
  element, 14
lecture courses, psychology major
  element, 14

letters of recommendations, graduate
  school, 43
libraries, internship resource, 35

M

market research analyst, career, 66–67
marriage counselor, career, 60
media buyer (advertising), career, 64
media planner (advertising), career, 65
mental health counselor, career, 60
mentors
  graduate school selection
    element, 41
  networking opportunity, 38
motivation, employee characteristic, 46

N

NAADAC (National Association for
  Addiction Professionals), 59
National Assembly, internship
  resource, 35
National Association for Addiction
  Professionals (NAADAC), 59
National Association of Colleges and
  Employers, desirable characteristics, 46
National Career Development
  Association (NCDA), 59
National Honor Society in Psychology
  (Psi Chi), 33, 106–107
National Honor Society in Psychology
  for Community and Junior Colleges
  (Psi Beta), 107
National Rehabilitation Counseling
  Association (NRCA), 61
NCDA (National Career Development
  Association), 59
neighbors, job market resource, 50
networking
  clubs/organizations, 32–33
  fellow students, 36–37
  graduate school selection
    element, 41

networking *(continued)*
    information interviews, 37–38
    internships, 33–35
    job market resource, 50–51
    mentors, 38
    shadowing programs, 37
    volunteering, 33, 35–36
neuropsychologist, career, 63, 64
non-profit organizations, internship
    opportunity, 34
NRCA (National Rehabilitation
    Counseling Association), 61

O

Occupational Outlook Handbook
    (Bureau of Labor Statistics), 11, 70
on-campus recruiters, job market
    resource, 51–52
O'NET, career particulars research
    site, 70
online applications, colleges/
    universities, 27
organizational psychologist, career, 63
organizations
    college selection element, 26
    job market resource, 52–53
    networking opportunity, 32–33

P

personality/character testing, major
    selection resource, 12
Peterson's Intercept Guide, 35
pharmacology course, psychology major
    integration, 15
police officer, career, 67
practicum. *See* internships
Princeton's Guide to Colleges, 24
professions, job market resource, 51
professor, graduate degree
    requirement, 39
Psi Beta (National Honor Society in
    Psychology for Community and
    Junior Colleges), 107
Psi Chi (National Honor Society in
    Psychology), 33, 106–107

psychology major
    directional paths, 18–19
    discussion courses, 14
    general skill requirements, 15–18
    introductory course, 13
    IUPUI survey questions, 13
    job outlook, 20
    laboratory courses, 14
    lecture courses, 14
    reasons for popularity, 7
    related courses, 15
    research methodology, 14
    seminar courses, 14
    statistics, 14
    thesis courses, 14
psychology paraprofessional, career, 67
psychotherapist, career, 63, 64
public relations specialist, career, 67

Q

questions
    college selection, 23–24
    college selection criteria, 25–27
    graduate school selection
        considerations, 40–41
    interview guidelines, 55–56
    psychology survey, 13

R

range of studies, college selection
    element, 26
receptions, networking opportunity,
    32–33
recommendations, graduate school, 43
recruiters, job market resource, 51–52
rehabilitation counselor, career, 60
research department, college selection
    element, 25
research methodology, psychology major
    element, 14
researcher, graduate degree
    requirement, 39
resumes
    class planning element, 32
    preparation guidelines, 47–48

retail buyer, career, 68
retail store manager, career, 68
rutgers University, career listings, 69–70

S

school psychologist
    case study, 100–104
    graduate degree requirement, 39
self-confidence, employee
  characteristic, 46
seminar courses, psychology major
  element, 14
seminars, networking opportunity,
  32–33
senior thesis, class planning element,
  31–32
shadowing programs, networking
  opportunity, 37
skills/abilities
    major selection, 10
    psychology major requirements,
      15–18
social psychologist
    career, 63, 64
    graduate degree requirement, 39
social services director, graduate degree
  requirement, 39
social services organizations, internship
  opportunity, 34
social worker, graduate degree
  requirement, 39
sociology course, psychology major
  integration, 15
sports psychologist, case study, 78–84
statistics course, psychology major
  element, 14
*Step Ahead to Your Future: A guide to
  choosing majors & careers* (IUPUI), 12
students
    job market resource, 50
    networking opportunity, 36–37
student-to-faculty ratio, college selection
  element, 25

T

teacher, career, 68–69
teaching assistant, internship
  opportunity, 34
teamwork skills, desirable employee
  characteristic, 46
thesis, class planning element, 31–32
thesis courses, psychology major
  element, 14
timeliness, interview importance, 55
transfers, college selection guidelines, 28

U

University of Kansas, Academic Majors
  Career Resources, 70
University of North Carolina, career
  listings, 70
University of Tennessee, career
  listings, 70
University of Texas, career listings, 70

V

values, major selection, 10
Vault.com, company overviews, 53–54
volunteering
    major selection resource, 12
    networking opportunity, 33,
      35–36

W

Web pages
    college selection resource, 22–23
    job-related Web sites, 49
women's studies class, psychology major
  integration, 15
work ethic, desirable employee
  characteristic, 46
workshops, major selection resource, 12

NOTES

NOTES

NOTES